The Death of a Child

The Death of a Child

Reflections for Grieving Parents

Elaine E. Stillwell

ACTA

ASSISTING CHRISTIANS TO ACT

PUBLICATIONS

The Death of a Child
Reflections for Grieving Parents
by Elaine E. Stillwell

Edited by Todd J. Behme and Gregory F. Augustine Pierce
Cover design by Tom A. Wright
Typesetting by Desktop Edit Shop, Inc.

Scripture quotations are from the New Revised Standard Version of the Bible, copyright © 1989 by the Division of Christian Education of the National Council of the Churches of Christ in the U.S.A. Used with permission. All rights reserved.

Published by: ACTA Publications
            Assisting Christians To Act
            4848 N. Clark Street
            Chicago, IL 60640-4711
            773-271-1030
            www.actapublications.com

Library of Congress Card Number: 2003115216

ISBN: 0-87946-260-4

Printed in the United States of America

Year: 10 09 08 07 06 05 04

Printing: 10 9 8 7 6 5 4 3 2 1

Contents

Dedication

To my husband, Joe, always at my side — ready to walk through fire for me and filling my days with love, laughter, happiness and lots of hugs.

To my daughter Annie, who chooses life with the tenacity of a true Taurus, making me so proud of her.

To my grandson Christopher, a ray of sunshine in my life, reminding me that joy still happens.

And in memory of my children Peggy and Denis, who continue to make a difference in the world as I sing their song.

Beginning the Journey

I can do all things through him who strengthens me.
Philippians 4:13

In an instant my life changed forever when my two oldest children, 21-year-old Denis and 19-year-old Peggy, were killed in a freak car accident August 2, 1986, not far from our home on Long Island.

Peggy died instantly; Denis was rushed into brain surgery. As my husband and I made arrangements for Peggy's wake and funeral, we ran back and forth between the funeral parlor and the intensive care unit where Denis clung to life. He was a tall, strong, healthy, athletic lifeguard. We truly believed he would survive and be ready for his junior year of college in a few weeks. But the day after we buried Peggy, Denis was declared brain dead. After arranging a brief prayer service at his bedside and signing the papers to donate his organs, my husband and I dried our tears, took deep sighs and, leaning on each other, faced our second funeral in one week. Once again I bombarded heaven with prayer, begging for strength and inspiration as I prepared another eulogy and Mass, choosing hymns and readings echoing Denis' distinct personality, just as I had for Peggy. Even in my state of shock and numbness, and fighting the utter weariness that assaulted my body, I was consumed with a passionate energy, because it was so important for me to tell the world how much I loved these children. I poured my heart and soul into preparing their funerals with every ounce of strength I could muster, thinking they would be my last gift of love to them. I never realized how many gifts of love would follow over the years to come.

As the last guest and all our caretakers left after Denis' funeral, my husband, Joe (my children's stepfather), and I sat there in the living room, staring at each other, thinking: *Where do we go from here? How do we get up in the morning? How do we sit at the dinner table with two vacant seats, soon to be three when our one remaining child leaves to begin her freshman year in college? How do we bear the utter quietness in our house after living with the constant din of telephone calls, stereos and chatter? How do we face the world again?* These were all frightening, overwhelming, almost paralyzing thoughts in those dark, beginning moments of unimaginable grief.

Facing the unbearable journey of bereaved parent, little did I know how much there was for me to learn about grieving.

How devastating it was to find there were no shortcuts or magic formulas to spare our pain. Facing the unbearable journey of bereaved parent, little did I know how much there was for me to learn about grieving. My life-renewing education—Grief 101, as I call it—began in 1986, a time when very little support material and few bereavement support groups were available, especially for parents who had lost a child. Now, years later, with a heart filled with helpful ideas gleaned from many sources, I want to share with you the life-giving lessons I have learned and shared with people all over the United States through my speaking, writing, group facilitating, and work with The Compassionate Friends, a self-help group for bereaved parents and siblings.

As bereaved parents we know the excruciating pain of losing a child, the constant struggle to gain control of our life again, and the stinging frustration of dealing with people who don't or might not want to understand what we are experiencing. In our personal agony we earnestly search for loving listeners and ways to help us create a "new normal" in our lives. As we adjust and improvise our daily routines, attempting to cope and survive, miraculously we begin to find joy in our tears and live life more fully.

Each grieving parent travels a different journey, but each journey presents a variety of opportunities—an amazing path designed by the Lord that keeps unfolding—helping us survive the death of our child and lead a meaningful life again. Never did I dream of the varied stepping-stones that would form my healing path, filling my life with abundant love, excitement, adventure and meaning. From founding a chapter of The Compassionate Friends, to becoming a state regional coordinator for the group, to being called to serve on the board of the National Catholic Ministry to the Bereaved, to speaking at and chairing national grief seminars and conferences, writing for national magazines and authoring books and pamphlets for the bereaved, to becoming the Bereavement Coordinator for the Diocese of Rockville Centre, New York, I could never have ever imagined the array of joys that would light up my life after suffering the deaths of Peggy and Denis. I did not have a master plan, but the Lord did! Everything I have ever learned—through my education, hobbies, talents or career—is used in the ministry I do today. And to my delight, the plan is still unfolding.

Grief work demands action in order for us to grow fully into the new person we become.

As you turn the pages, notice that chapter titles and subheadings begin with active words, because grief work demands action in order for us to grow fully into the new person we become.

May you discover new rays of light to illuminate your journey as a parent who has lost your beloved child, and may your heart gently open to the joys of life again.

I will instruct you and teach you the way you should go;
I will counsel you with my eye upon you.

Psalm 32:8

Creating a "New Normal"

I will give you a new heart
and place a new spirit within you.

Ezekiel 36:26

Discovering our life has changed forever

My heart felt like it was being crushed in a vise, and my energy level left me feeling paralyzed, unable to do the things I used to do. I was the typical bereaved parent, facing an endless new day and yearning to be the old me, the person who laughed, loved, enjoyed life, and surrounded myself with friends, hobbies and work. I desperately wanted my life to remain what it was before Peggy and Denis died, but I was foolish to think that was possible. For we parents who have lost a child, life has changed forever, and there is a gaping hole in our hearts that will always be part of who we are.

Our immediate work—and grieving is hard work, make no mistake about that—is moving the love we have for our child from the outside to the inside. As painful as it is to no longer be able to see, hear or touch our child physically, we must learn to feel our child as part of our heart forever, knowing that love never dies. This requires patience and time. There are no short-cuts and no timetables. Each grieving parent must go at his or her own pace and listen to his or her own heart; there is no one way. Grief is the price we pay for having loved, and our pain is none other than the result of the joy with which our children have blessed us.

No matter what age child we lost, we parents feel cheated of the many hopes and dreams we had for him or her. If we lost a child through miscarriage or stillbirth, we never even experience the joy of getting to know them. If an infant or baby died, we no longer have that dependent child to care for, nurture, play with or cuddle. If we spent months running from doctor to doctor or at the bedside of a young child, we feel the weight of not being needed anymore. If we lost a troubled teenager—acting out, rebellious, involved with drugs or the wrong crowd, tied up with legal entanglements—a sense of guilt overpowers us, with our mind replaying the theme, *What could I have done differently?* If we argued or had violent disagreements with an adult child who died, there may be unfinished business that cannot be resolved—at least in the normal way.

> *We might be very hard on ourselves, suffering waves of enormous guilt. We may be angry — with God, with ourselves, even with our deceased child.*

We might be very hard on ourselves, suffering waves of enormous guilt. We may be angry—with God, with ourselves, even with our deceased child. We may be overcome with a sadness we just cannot seem to shake.

We take inventory of our situation and ask ourselves what we need to make the rest of our days have some meaning. Each of us will have a different list and a different design for survival.

Creating a "new normal" is hard. The secret is to have a plan, no matter how simple.

Finding the motivation to go on

Many of us feel as if we want to jump into the grave to be with our child. This is a very normal feeling, but I promise you it dissipates over time. We don't really want to die; we just want to be out of the excruciating pain we are suffering. What do you do when you are filled with pain that goes right down to your toes? How do you handle grief so raw that all days seem like bad days, with some worse than others?

After the busyness of the wake, funeral or other farewell ritual, and still reeling from shock and numbness, we are left to find a reason to get out of bed in the morning, to get back in the swing of things, to be part of the world again. When you are hurting so badly, wanting to go on with life takes great motivation.

Answering how he lived through the horrors of the death camps, Holocaust survivor and psychotherapist Viktor Frankl replied that you have to have a goal. He said that his goal for the rest of his life was to "tell the world." So it is with us bereaved parents—to survive we need to tell the world about our child. This is a healthy, realistic goal, and it is the first step in healing, according to many support books and grief counselors. It might take us a little time to figure out this first step, but eventually, telling our child's story will be a source of great comfort and healing to us.

Going through my children's possessions, emptying out wallets, cleaning out drawers and sorting clothing, I had the sickening feeling that as I discarded credit cards, social security cards, college IDs and driver's licenses I was somehow *erasing* my children. I was so afraid of forgetting any details of their lives. Remembering is a serious worry for most bereaved parents. We want to be able to recall our child's voice, laughter, walk, smile, eyes, dimples, hair, hugs—every little thing that made him or her unique. How we want to memorize it all. Miraculously, we seem to minimize or block out unpleasant or problematic memories, and we all have a few of those. How quickly "teenage syndrome" problems can disappear from our thoughts, for example, after an older child dies.

The dam of pleasant recollections overflows and floods our mind, and we are left to create new ways to keep these memories alive. We have become the "keeper of the memories," and it is our job to never let our child be forgotten. We adopt a special mantra: "If their song is to continue, then we must do the singing." This was a powerful motivator for me. I didn't have a clue how I was going to make sure the memory of Peggy and Denis would never be erased from people's minds, but the idea was planted and would blossom later.

Thinking of them every waking minute and during sleepless nights, I also realized I wanted them to remember me as the mom they loved and someone who was fun for them to be with. How I wanted them to be proud of me and the life I was leading. I wanted them to be looking down from heaven on me with their buttons popping as they exclaimed, "That's my mom," instead of being embarrassed and disappointed that I wouldn't come out from under the covers. That simple motive, vividly pictured in my mind, replayed day after day, forced me out of bed every morning to face each new day and the various phases of grief that engulfed me unannounced.

I also was determined not to waste the special love I had for my two deceased children. I promised myself I would find ways to use it, never dreaming of all the possibilities that would cross my path in future years. Every time I share that special love, I keep their memories alive. People still tell me today that they feel as if they know Denis and Peggy, even though they never met them, and that makes my heart sing. Using that special love, doing things in their name, powerfully touches many lives, including my own.

I was armed with three solid reasons to get up each day:
- Keeping my children from being erased from people's minds.
- Doing everything I could to make them proud of me.
- Not wasting the special love I had for them.

Making choices

We bereaved parents learn that we constantly have choices to make. In the early dark days of our grief, we face a basic choice: lie down and give up or fight to stay alive and lead a meaningful life as a tribute to our child. Even though we feel confused, angry, exhausted, lifeless, empty and sorrowful, making simple decisions such as what to wear and what to eat each day lays the groundwork for making more important choices. With each decision we make, with each baby step we take, we grow stronger and begin to take back control of our life.

Starting with little things, we gather strength and confidence for bigger things. Give yourself permission to go step by step, rather than having someone else make all the choices or try to "fix" your grief. Allow yourself time to find choices that give your heart a moment's peace, whether it's a cup of tea with a friend, a savored time to meditate, a leisurely walk with the dog, a link with nature, soothing music, comforting prayers, crying, sighing, jogging, hugging or playing with grandchildren. Keep a list of the life-renewing activities that give you solace and rescue yourself on a bad day by returning to one or more of them.

Choice after choice, we attempt to re-enter the world that—shockingly to us—is still going on, even though our child is dead. Sometimes carrying on our regular daily schedule keeps us busy and moving without requiring too much planning or exertion on our part. We just keep doing the things that are familiar to us, often in a robotic way. Other times, because our child was so much a part of our daily routine (especially if he or she was an only child), we have to develop a whole new daily plan that fits our energy level and our grieving pattern. Some newly bereaved parents are up at the crack of dawn and others stir at noon. Some make it out of bed, some get as far as the couch, and others gingerly attempt to add new things to their daily schedule. Taking things a step at a time, we move forward inch by inch, doing what we can handle and eliminating or cutting back on those things that are just too hard for us right now. Some of us thrive on cooking, while others would rather starve than face a kitchen or a grocery store. Some stay busy and energize themselves by dusting, polishing, and vacuuming; others couldn't care less if the house fell down around them.

Taking things a step at a time, we move forward inch by inch, doing what we can handle and eliminating or cutting back on those things that are just too hard for us right now.

Everything we parents of children who have died do to keep going is done by trial and error, trying to discover what works for us. We have to experiment a little to find out what refreshes our spirit or permits us to breathe easier—without that gut-wrenching pain that only we know. We all must learn the important lesson of honoring our feelings and operating on our own timetable. We learn there is no right or wrong way to grieve. We choose to do whatever helps us feel even the least bit alive again. Many of us learn to pamper ourselves, not out of selfishness but out of wisdom, because we discover we cannot be good to anyone else unless we are good to ourselves. This is a very hard lesson for those of us who are used to putting everyone else first.

We choose to do whatever helps us feel even the least bit alive again.

So try some new things that develop new pleasures for yourself or your loved ones, whether it's rearranging the furniture, developing new hobbies, creating different ways to celebrate the holidays, making new friends, doing all the things you always put off, or just taking time to smell the roses. I found comfort in doing things my children loved to do: walking the beach, listening to music, watching *Saturday Night Live,* rooting for Notre Dame, relaxing with a good movie, making chocolate chip cookies, eating French toast, and decorating the Christmas tree.

As much as we would like it, there are no buttons to push for an easy solution. We have to keep looking for the things that talk to our heart, even in a whisper. What works for you might not work for me and vice versa, because we all grieve differently. As time goes on, however, our rescue list gets longer and longer as we discover more and more ways to open our hearts to life.

Building structure

If we had a job when our child died, we need to determine when we feel strong enough to return to work. Some parents might find it necessary to apply for an extended leave of absence. Others might be forced back to the workplace immediately because of financial pressures.

I went back to work as a third-grade teacher three weeks after burying Peggy and Denis. It was the beginning of the school year, and every teacher knows how important it is to greet your class, set down the ground rules, and make it *your class*. Going back to work was a very good move for me. The routine, the love of the children, and the quick pace of each day saved my life. Working gave structure to my day, got me out of our too-quiet house, and made me feel needed by my students and appreciated by my colleagues. My work was like a gift to me—giving me purpose, making me follow a routine, and rapidly turning the pages of the calendar.

Many parents experience these same feelings after returning to work. Unfortunately, some are merely trying to escape the tears and black-cloud feelings of their households. Some work unnecessarily long hours to avoid dealing with the overwhelming grief of their spouses.

I was grateful for my husband's tender understanding. Joe and I had been married only two years at the time, and I'm sure he felt as if he had lost his bubbly bride along with two of his dear stepchildren. By the time I would get home from work and sit down in my recliner, which I called my "thinking chair," I would be exhausted. Tears would flood my face. I didn't even have to think of Peggy and Denis. The tears—the ones I had kept in check all day—would flow freely. It was a blessed release, and I thanked God for it. An hour later Joe, whom I called "my blotter" because he soaked up all those tears, would gently inquire, "What's for dinner?" He made me smile as he'd give me a hug and help set the table, and we'd chat about our day. He respected my need to cry and gave me my space, but also, most importantly, he connected with me in such gentle ways. I had the warm, wonderful feeling that he was always there for me. He never said, "Enough already." Instead he gave me the space and permission to grieve in my own way, which was quite different from his. That daily routine of releasing the ache that had built up during the day was as vital as breathing for me as I struggled to create a "new normal" for myself.

> *That daily routine of releasing the ache that had built up during the day was as vital as breathing for me as I struggled to create a "new normal" for myself.*

Telling our head

After reading a few books on grief, I realized how important it was to fill my head with positive thoughts. I learned "it's what you tell your head" that counts. If I got up every day and thought I would never see my children again, my stomach would do flip-flops and be filled with butterflies. However, if I told myself each morning that I was one day closer to seeing my children again, my heart would jump for joy. What a difference!

Reading about a young widow who had lost her husband in a motorcycle accident, I was moved by her simple response to the unrelenting question of all grieving parents: *Why?* She said simply, "God knows why, and that's good enough for me."

Counting our blessings is a great lesson.

Why didn't I think of that, I thought enviously. Then I happily added to myself, *And he is going to tell me the answer someday.* That simple thought made me feel much better. It was a lot less painful than beating myself up every day with an unanswerable question. Now I believe that one day God will take me in his loving embrace and I'll finally learn why my children died. And it probably won't even seem important anymore!

Looking at a half-filled glass, do we see it as half full or half empty? Counting our blessings is a great lesson. It opens our eyes to what we still have, what has graced our lives, and what resources there are to help us along our journey of grief. Someone said to me, "You've had a hard life, but you have a good life." I thought, *That's it in a nutshell.* Emphasizing what we have, rather than what has been taken from us, empowers us to keep going, to keep nurturing all the positive things we have in our life. That's why gratitude journals have become popular among the bereaved. They help us keep in mind the blessings we do enjoy even in the midst of our sorrow.

As bereaved parents our life has changed forever, but it has not ended. We might feel lost, walking in unfamiliar territory. We might even need a new road map or new anchors. But we can learn that healing begins by listening to our own heart. In that quiet place, we can discover the peace of God that is always there for us to experience and to rely upon. God is guiding us to new possibilities that we never would have recognized ourselves. Creating a "new normal" takes courage and work, but it is possible!

In the shadow of your wings, I will take refuge
until the destroying storms pass by.

Psalm 57:1

Baring Our Soul

I loathe my life; I will give free utterance to my complaint;
I will speak from the bitterness of my soul.

Job 10:1

Finding those loving people

Grieving is hard work for everyone, but even more so for bereaved parents. It is not to be done alone. Finding people who are there for us as "loving listeners" and who put no restrictions on us is a priority. We learn very quickly that we need people who will give us permission to grieve as long and as loud as we need. We don't have the energy to spar with relatives and friends who tell us what we should do. It is too upsetting to argue or to have to defend our actions when we are sorting out our own feelings and trying to face life without our child. No wonder the number one complaint of parents who have lost a child of any age is the insensitive remarks made by others. They are usually offered with good intentions but spoken in ignorance, and they can be devastating.

Our loving listeners can be family or friends—and might even be people we never dreamed would enter our lives to accompany us on our journey. Our heart knows right away who the people are who make us feel better. They are the ones we choose to encircle us with their love and caring ways. They are the ones who will protect and shield us from the harsh outside world as we struggle to regain our strength, find our focus, and get back on our feet. For example, the parents of a lifeguard who worked with my son, a priest we met at a friend's wedding, a new neighbor who lost a son, people who read our story in the newspaper and other bereaved parents we met in our support group became a vital part of Joe's and my lives.

Loving listeners give us time to deal with our grief by letting us feel our loss, not minimizing it or ignoring it, and not trying to "fix" it. Their attitude prevents our grief from being short-circuited—to explode at a later date. When we feel comfortable with the people surrounding us, we can give ourselves permission to cry, releasing pent-up anxiety. We can talk about our child, look at pictures, share stories, make some decisions— all important steps in healing. We can feel a sense of peace and of hope. We don't have to put on a happy face and say we are fine when our heart is breaking. We can be true to ourselves and what we feel.

Surrounding ourselves with loving listeners gives us time to discover our own needs. It also allows us to feel the positive reinforcement and encouragement they provide. They are giving us permission to grieve, and that is a welcome gift. We need a safe place and safe people with whom to grieve.

Sometimes we have to stay at arm's length from those who are too demanding or insensitive to our needs, and this could include close relatives. Just because they are related to us does not mean they are open to understanding our pain or willing to know what we need. When I suggested to a relative that he read a grief book to understand my pain, he said he'd rather read a book on golf. He was being brutally honest, but it was really his way of telling me he couldn't handle my pain.

Relatives might be crippled from their own pain about our child's death, or they may simply wish to make their own lives less uncomfortable by filling us with unwanted advice and demands for a quick recovery. We don't have to avoid these people forever—just until we are strong enough to deal with them and to be able to explain our needs to them. We can mend fences later!

Telling the world how we really feel

We bereaved parents need the freedom to tell our story again and again. The more we talk about our dead child, the more the child becomes part of our heart and the sooner we begin to deal with the reality of the loss.

Friends suggested I get medication to ease my pain after the death of my children, but my doctor wouldn't even give me an aspirin. He said, "Elaine, you're a talker, just keep talking and you'll feel better." He was right; talking was healing medicine for me. No matter where I was—in a grocery line, at the bank, in a department store, at the airport, walking the dog—I told the world about my children, whether they wanted to hear about them or not! Many times I left people with open mouths, speechless, not knowing how to respond to the loss of two children. But I was consumed with passion to tell everybody about Denis and Peggy because I was terrified that they would be forgotten. At the time I didn't even realize how healing talking was for me. It was therapy, sharing my loss while making me accept that my children were no longer physically here. The grief books say that when we share our sorrow we divide the pain and that when we share our joy we double the joy. I found that formula to be true.

Grief books say that when we share our sorrow we divide the pain and that when we share our joy we double the joy. I found that formula to be true.

Many bereaved parents, of course, do need counseling or a combination of professional help and medication to begin their healing. They should seek this without the slightest bit of embarrassment or guilt or delay. (If you cannot afford counseling or medicine, don't be afraid to ask relatives, friends or even your clergy to help. Most will understand and be willing to get you in touch with the right resources. People always ask what they can do to help, and this would be one case where accepting their aid is both necessary and urgent.)

Even though it is hard for us grieving parents to admit or even explain to others the extent of our pain, we do a disservice to ourselves and to the people who ask how we are if we sugarcoat our reply. How will others know how it feels to lose a child if *we* don't level with them? How will they know how to help us if *we* don't tell them?

Don't be upset if you are tongue-tied. In the early days of our loss, most of us find it is just too hard, too painful, or too much trouble to bare our soul and tell people how we really feel. It's easier and less complicated to say "Fine" or "As well as can be expected." Besides, we can't even find words to describe the excruciating pain we are feeling, so we sidestep the issue. When we're innocently asked how many children we have, we

We have to discover exactly what our needs are, and then we have to get the courage to communicate them.

fill up with raw emotion, have pain in our stomach, and squirm to find the right phrases. Crying a lot and feeling exhausted, we feel isolated and estranged from the world. We don't feel like mingling or talking. We need time to get our bearings. We take the easy way out, pretending we are "fine." We just don't have the energy or the words to explain how we really feel. But that will come in time.

It takes ten times the usual energy to get through a day as we grieve. We are worn out just trying to stay alive, attempting to stay afloat in the new, unfamiliar world of being a bereaved parent. Struggling with little energy and fighting the utter exhaustion of grieving is frustrating, and not being able to do all the things we are used to doing, or wanting to do, sends us a crystal-clear message: "Let others help."

We have to discover exactly what our needs are, and then we have to get the courage to communicate them. Do we need food delivered, a babysitter, a hug, a comforting book, a listener, a sympathetic card, a phone call, help with paperwork or shopping, a ride to the store? Figuring this out takes time and patience. Then we need the strength to put the right words together, to feel comfortable with the message we want to deliver. It's only by trial and error that we come up with honest responses to the familiar questions and irritating comments that bombard our aching heart, such as:

- "What's the matter?" *My child died.* (A lot of parents can't even say the word "died.")
- "Snap out of it; it's been months; you've got to get on with your life." *Just walk one day in my shoes.*
- "Call me when you need me." *I do need you: Do*

my grocery shopping; walk the dog; mow the lawn; send dinner over.

- "God needed another angel." *I need my child.*
- "Why are you still grieving?" *My child is still dead.*
- "You will have closure after the funeral and burying your child." *I won't have closure until they close the lid on my own casket.*

Some people who have never lost a loved one, especially a child, don't seem to understand the depth of the pain and the time needed to create a "new normal." They don't realize that no matter what milestone event we attend, our child will be physically missing from it. Even though we are happy for our relatives and friends, it can be very painful for us to watch the graduate receive his or her diploma, the father of the bride dance with his daughter, or the mother of the groom dance with her son. We ache to have those pleasures with our child. Our sorrow accompanies us for a lifetime and can be triggered unannounced.

Part of our ongoing education as a grieving parent is to share what we learn about grief. I call it "teaching the world;" others refer to it as teaching the "civilians" or the "aliens," meaning people who have not suffered this particularly devastating loss and don't have a clue how to deal with those who have. Relatives, friends, neighbors and coworkers can all learn from us how to "be there" for those who grieve. We have to tell our friends and family that we love to hear our child's name mentioned, that it's healing to talk about our child, music to our ears when others share stories about our child, and comforting to receive cards and phone calls on our child's birthday and anniversary of death, sometimes lovingly referred to as his or her "heaven date." And flowers are always welcome! Our hearts need to know that our child is not forgotten—especially after the first couple of years.

Parents of students I taught have thanked me for being so open with my class when a death affected one of the children—whether it was a grandparent, parent, sibling, friend or even a pet. My students learned that death is part of life and that there are positive, practical things you can do to reach out to the person who is hurting. Whether the class drew heartfelt cards, wrote simple poetry, or listened to the bereaved student tell wonderful memories, it gave them a lifelong model for grieving.

Denis' birthday is in February. For the rest of my career after his death, I wouldn't assign homework on that special day. My third-graders, grateful to him for rescuing them from homework that night, would clap their hands and raise their arms in a cheering gesture while chanting, "We love Denis!" Do you know what that did for my heart? By sharing the special occasion of my firstborn's birthday with my class, it became a date they looked forward to. They even told their younger brothers and sisters, future students of mine, that they would never have homework on February 4. How disappointed they all were to learn Peggy was born in August!

Telling the world how we really feel can have some rewarding moments, especially when we feel the loving support of those we have educated and see them no longer afraid to reach out to the newly bereaved.

Tuning in to our spouse

Feelings need to be shared, especially among family members. Because we all grieve differently, we need to know where everybody else is coming from. Rarely are we on the same page. None of us are mind readers, so we need to share what helps and what hurts us. We want to keep the doors of communication open to prevent the pain of isolation as we struggle with our individual grief.

Ways of grieving vary within families. Some family members cry a lot; others shed no tears. Some can't leave the house; others are never home. Some can't answer the phone; others can't put it down. Some attempt a daily routine; others can't get out of bed. Some have a social life; others would not consider it. Some are very introspective, searching for answers; others are filled with rage. Some find solace in their faith; others refuse to talk to God. Different ways of grieving can seem to create an invisible wall that separates us at a time when we desperately need togetherness. We can feel that we are living a million miles apart even though we live in the same house. We have to try to be like kids in a sandbox, all there together but each building something different, reflecting our precious individuality.

For couples, staying connected is important. We must give each other mental and emotional support by respecting individual ways of grieving. We have to work at making time to be with each other, even when we feel as if we're living on different planets. Avoiding blame and sharing our daily ups and downs helps keep communication channels open. Being honest about our feelings is important, whether it's talking about what to do with our child's room, pushy relatives, missing friends, social invitations, a possible vacation, or things we are not able to face yet. Sexual issues need to be discussed and feelings shared, since interest and desire can vary for each partner. Rejection of intimacy just adds to the suffering that already exists. Some partners need very clear space, while others need their spouse's loving arms wrapped around them, infusing them with strength to face each new day. There is no rule of thumb, but we all need mutual respect, honoring how we feel, even if we don't fully understand our spouse's emotional needs.

We have to try to be there for each other on our good days, and we must not leave our partner isolated when we're both having a bad day.

We often wish our spouse reacted to everything exactly as we do, but it doesn't seem to work that way. It's more like a see-saw—while one is feeling up, the other is feeling down; and if one jumps off, the other suffers a painful crash. We have to try to be there for each other on our good days, and we must not leave our partner isolated when we're both having a bad day. Grieving couples have to give each other space to come to grips with their own soul-searching issues, to work out their own solutions, to do trial-and-error experimentation to learn what works for them. We have to let our spouse know we are close by, that we do love him or her, that we need a gentle embrace and touch more than ever. Most of all, we need our partner's permission to grieve. Although Joe and I grieved differently, we found solace in sitting in our family room together, not necessarily having to speak, listening to the evening news or perhaps a concert on TV, sometimes just holding hands or blowing a kiss across the room. When I found comforting grief articles that I wanted to share with him, he listened patiently to every one of them. Honoring each other's lifelines invited togetherness—whether it was through reading, writing, music, meditation, socialization, gardening, sports or the family pet. Sheltered in each other's arms at night, Joe and I affirmed our mutual need for each other and gathered strength to face the next day.

Bereaved mothers and fathers both need moral support.

When we are desperate for our partner's support and it's not there, we become angry. We feel hurt, misunderstood and unloved. These feelings make it even harder for us to help each other. It is almost impossible to lean on our spouse when he or she is already bent in two with grief. Sometimes we have to turn to other people to "walk the walk" with us. That's when those loving people make a huge difference in our life—just being there when we need support.

Bereaved mothers and fathers both need moral support. In my experience, many men focus on tasks rather than feelings. They will try to plod on without asking for support or how to give it. Most women, on the other hand, feel free to express their feelings and often have a circle of friends to hear them out. People reinforce these masculine/feminine tendencies each time someone asks, "How is your wife doing?" The man thinks, "Hey, I'm the father. Why don't you care how I feel?" We are all human. We all want our loss recognized. It adds to our burden of grief to be left out of the loop. We need to hear out our spouse's feelings, and it's equally important to express to our partner how we feel. Remember, human beings are not mind readers. Both the bereaved father and mother must feel that they have been heard—maybe not understood, but at least respected.

We also have to face the fact that our child's death changes our relationship with our spouse forever. As we struggle with our grief, together and alone, our relationship can either be weakened or grow stronger. Our actions determine that choice.

Sharing with our remaining children

Our remaining children, the bereaved siblings, are hurting too. It is important for us parents to model our grief for them, letting them know that we grieve and that it's healthy to grieve. When we cry, we are telling them it's all right to cry. When we talk about their brother or sister, we are sending a message that it's OK to say the name and repeat the stories over and over, keeping precious memories alive. By showing our children it's all right to grieve, we give them permission to grieve openly and to share what is in their hearts.

Including surviving siblings in the funeral preparations and the ceremony or memorial service validates their loss. They had a relationship, different from ours, that needs to be honored. They may suffer from "survivor guilt," feeling guilty that they remain alive, or they may be plagued by hurtful comments they might have screamed in anger at their sibling before the tragedy even happened. They may be upset because of some unfinished business or hurting from the need to call out one more time the rarely voiced words "I love you" to their sibling.

In some cases, just the change in birth-order position—being left as an only child or suddenly becoming the oldest or youngest in the family, for example—can bring new status and responsibilities to our remaining children. Their attempts to "fill in" for the dead sibling can make them question their own worth and self-esteem—which can be painful, confusing and frustrating. Missing the "buddy" they palled around with or shared a room with, teased and fought with, watched TV with, played sports with, can leave a big void in their life. Grappling with all these feelings is a monumental, ongoing task for siblings. Their whole world has changed too.

We learn the hard way that children grieve differently than we do. They grieve in spurts—usually much shorter spurts than parents. They can be crying and unable to get out of bed one minute, and the next instant they'll be out the door to play basketball or ride bikes or mix with friends. It's vital to give them space, but also to include them in talking, sharing feelings, and making family plans. We have to do our best not to overprotect them out of fear that something could happen to them as well. (Telling my remaining child, Annie, that she was "statistically untouchable" became a bittersweet family joke with us, but it gave her the freedom to pursue her dreams and not feel boxed in by overprotective parents. With our blessing, and despite the unsolicited opinions that she, my husband and I got from many others that she should stay home with us, Annie left for her freshman year of college three weeks after burying her sister and brother.)

Allow time for you and your surviving children to grieve together.

We must make our home a safe place for our other children to grieve, with no timetables or pressure to get on with their life. We should provide a relaxed atmosphere that will allow them to express their feelings—a safe place for them to grieve, not one in constant turmoil. Allow time for you and your surviving children to grieve together. Share helpful books, articles, poems and music. (E-mail was not available to me in 1986, but I made sure there was a letter in Annie's college mailbox every day, and many of them contained copies of something I had read that I thought would be helpful to her.) Guide your children to the children's department or the adult grief section of a bookstore or public library, where there are to be found beautiful stories with uplifting messages for their grieving hearts. Suggest they keep a journal to record their daily feelings; naming their feelings helps them deal with them. A simple black and white notebook will do, or give them one of the elegant journals that are popular today. Introduce them to a support group for people their age. Helping them find a buddy who understands the pain and sadness of losing a sibling allows a very healing experience of shared feelings to occur. When children relate to another person their age who feels exactly the same way they do—with similar thoughts, regrets and worries—it lifts an incredible burden of guilt off their shoulders. They suddenly realize they aren't the only ones to have such emotions. As hard as it is for us adults to accept, young people usually prefer to talk to other young people rather than to their parents. For one reason (which when you think about it is heroic on their part), they can tell their peers what they are really thinking and feeling without having to worry about adding to their parents' burden of grief.

Including our children in decisions about the possessions of their brother or sister opens up a dialogue as we sort out the items together. Choosing favorite photos—for framing, sending to relatives, or filling family "brag" books—offers time to share memories. Deciding what to do with the personal belongings and room of their sibling helps them deal with the reality of their loss. Picking one or more "linking" objects to keep for themselves keeps them connected in a special way. A favorite book, teddy bear, wristwatch, bracelet, sweatshirt, or baseball cap—even stereo, computer and sports equipment—can offer surviving siblings a sense of closeness, comforting feelings, and a replay of happy memories.

As we create a "new normal" in our life we have to find a balance that includes our new self, our spouse, our remaining children, and our child who died. This will take time and patience, and lots of love.

Linking with the clergy

Most of us bereaved parents turn to the clergy after the death of our child. They are among our first contacts. We are seldom looking for words of wisdom. There are no words to take away our pain. There are no answers. We simply need the rituals and prayers they can do so well.

Although many of us receive encouragement and support from clergy through the beautiful ceremonies surrounding our child's funeral, statistics show that few families get follow-up help from their clergy person after the funeral, no matter what the religion. If you are hurting because you have not heard from the clergy after the funeral, you are not alone. Sadly, this is the second-biggest complaint of bereaved parents (the first being insensitive remarks from well-meaning people).

Most of us want a clergy member to console us in our grief—to tell us we matter, that our loved ones matter, that God still loves us. We might feel a closeness to a priest or minister from a long association or simply from the poignant funeral he or she presided over for our child. Knowing someone cares, especially someone who acknowledges our pain as well as God's love, comforts us in our time of great sorrow. Being vulnerable and fragile and filled with so many unanswered questions, we appreciate linking with a loving listener from our faith tradition.

Whether we actively practice our religion or have not participated in many years, there is a part of us that yearns for its comfort and promises.

Whether we actively practice our religion or have not participated in many years, there is a part of us that yearns for its comfort and promises. Those bereaved parents with a faith-based community seem to do better in their grief than those who have none. However, the death of a child can also be a time when we question everything about our faith—when everything seems without meaning, when we feel totally abandoned by the God we love. This is quite normal and is part of the grief process. We need time to sort out our strong feelings and talk to God through prayer, meditation, reading, journaling—or just plain yelling and screaming.

The extended mourning period is a vital time when clergy can reach out to us instead of disappearing from our life. Important as a sounding board or perhaps to point us in the right direction, clergy can accompany us on our grief journey. Simply with their presence or ability to reinforce our beliefs, answer our questions, and pray with us, they can light the way for us to find a meaningful life again. Clergy can reinforce the gift of hope. Their accepting us without judgment and listening to our angry outbursts against God is more helpful than providing useless clichés and empty words. Clergy can offer suggestions for coping, recommend helpful books, refer us to support groups and counselors, invite us to lectures and commemorative rituals, or introduce us to someone who has suffered a similar loss and might give us hope and inspiration.

Our hearts want the clergy to take the time to visit us, to call us, to send us a note. We want them to validate our loss. Despite great faith in God, people still experience real pain from grief. How we want to feel the special embrace of our faith when we are so devastated, suffering the death of our child! (That's why I couldn't refuse the invitation to become bereavement coordinator for my diocese in 1998, even though I had recently retired from teaching after a 35-year career. I wanted those who grieve to feel the embrace of their parish and the caring of their clergy—a support I craved that was never extended to me after my children's funerals. I didn't want others to feel abandoned by the church in their loss. Now I am training bereavement ministers—both clergy and lay people—who are ready to accompany the bereaved on their grief journey.)

Clergy are not mind readers, either. Sometimes we have to tell them what we need if their response is inadequate or nonexistent. Sharing our needs with them, actually teaching them, can be a great eye-opener to those priests and ministers who have not realized or experienced the depth and many phases of a bereaved parent's grief. Some grieving parents, in their deepest sorrow, are unfortunately forced to turn elsewhere—to another parish or church or even to another faith—to find the healing compassion they need. As hard as that may be, it is a necessary step for some of us to find the powerful, nurturing embrace of faith for which our hearts and souls are longing. Finding another church is sometimes a more fruitful step than abandoning religion altogether and missing out on the spiritual satisfaction it provides.

Talking to God

Most grieving parents wonder: *Where is God? How could God let this happen? Why did God do this to me?* Some of us certainly find comfort in our faith, but others are very angry with God. Some reject him altogether.

Don't be afraid to talk to God about your thoughts and feelings. Feelings are neither right nor wrong. He can handle our anger, our doubts, our questions. Many of us mistakenly think we are angry at God when actually we are angry at reality. Expressing to God what is in our heart opens a healing dialogue, begins an invitation to reconciliation, and nurtures our desire to understand our loss.

Whatever we do, we need to keep talking. Telling our story over and over is the best medicine for healing, and sometimes God is the best or even the only listener who can handle our raw emotions. We can tell our story to God by simply talking. In fact, praying *is* talking—talking to God. In our own words or in those of a favorite prayer, we can converse with God, who is always there listening, night or day. Telling God our fears, our anger, our guilt, or anything else that bothers us, we can unload those heavy burdens by expressing them, instead of stuffing them down inside us to erupt and haunt us at a later date.

Being honest is important. We don't have to put on a happy face. We can say exactly what we feel. We can whisper or we can shout. God is always there for us, to carry us when we can no longer walk on our own. We can empty into him all the nagging, unanswerable questions that burden us.

With tenderness and love, God will guide us through our sorrow. We will feel new hope radiating within us as we bare our soul to him, telling him how we really feel. Unburdening our heart can bring us an inner peace that nourishes, heals and renews our spirit, and also opens us to accepting the divine plan unfolding in our life.

What better loving listener could we find? God knows the pain of the bereaved parent. After all, his only Son died a terrible death.

———————————

As a mother comforts her child, so I will comfort you.
Isaiah 66:13

Riding the Roller Coaster of Grief

God is our refuge and strength,
a very present help in trouble.

Psalm 46:1

Managing good days and bad days

Finding a reason to get up each day gets us bereaved parents moving—whether it is to give our spouse a "Good morning" kiss, make the kids' breakfast, walk the dog, attend church, or get to work. Structure allows us to do things automatically, without having to think. It makes the hours tick by a little faster, making our endless days peel off the calendar and our broken hearts feel a little stronger. With each passing day we find out more about ourselves — discovering what eases our pain and what adds to it. Taking these lessons to heart, we can keep a list of the things that help us breathe easier. Anything—no matter how trivial—that revives our spirit or eases our pain belongs on our "to do" list. As we create our "new normal," we are grateful for anything that helps us cope and survive.

It almost doesn't matter what we do; we just have to do something. Sharing our thoughts with a good friend, calling a telephone buddy, working in the garden, playing the piano, scrubbing the floor, writing in our journal, watching a football game, sewing, golfing, bike riding, jogging, playing racquetball, doing carpentry—whatever it is that lifts our burden for a few minutes is what we need to do. When we find something that delights us, we will do it a hundred times.

Roger Crawford, born with shortened arms and missing fingers and toes, said: "The only difference between you and me is that you can see my handicap, but I can't see yours. We all have them. When people ask me how I've been able to overcome my physical handicaps, I tell them that I haven't overcome anything. I've simply learned what I can't do—such as play the piano or eat with chopsticks—but more importantly, I've learned what I can do. Then I do what I can with all my heart and soul."

Like Roger Crawford, we have to discover what we *can* do and do it with all our heart and soul. It could be as simple as cutting a bouquet of flowers from our garden, saying the rosary or hitting a tennis ball. It could be as extensive as planning a grand memorial for our child. One dad spent the first year after his daughter's death designing her tombstone—researching the finest stone, finding the best stonecutter, selecting the right words to be etched on it, and actually renting a crane to set it in place himself. The project filled his days with purpose and his mind with something he could do that was dedicated to his dead child. He found something meaningful he could do that catapulted him into action and carried him through the darkest days.

Focusing on things we can do keeps us active and "out from under the covers."

Focusing on things we can do keeps us active and "out from under the covers." Some of us cook up a storm; others call their favorite take-out restaurant. Some curl up with a good grief support book; others escape into the world of the mystery novel. Some dive into mounting paperwork; others dip gingerly into writing in their journal. Some take long walks; others find the safety of their chaise lounge. Some escape by watching a rented movie; others spend hours arranging a photo album of their child. Some call for the support of their friends' presence; others relish sitting alone, getting in touch with their inner self. We all have to find what lifts us out of a slump and motivates us to keep going.

What ignites our spark of survival? Having a telephone buddy, someone we can call when we feel down, is a great help. Many of us make good friends at our support groups. Calling a friend—being able to vent about our frustrations, the loss of our dreams, or our feelings of being cheated—helps us deal with the painful feelings rather than letting those feelings control us. We feel so much better after unloading the thoughts that weigh us down. We don't have to be a prisoner of our feelings. All we have to do is pick up that telephone. Sharing our feelings divides the pain and opens our heart to new ideas. It's very simple: Just let the feelings out and the friends in!

On tough days we learn to take care of ourselves, to rest, to pamper ourselves, to conserve our energy, to refuel. We remind ourselves that we can make a brand-new start tomorrow. We lean into the grief, bending like trees in a hurricane. We bend to keep from breaking. We rearrange what's important to us—things we do, people we see, hobbies we pursue—to stay alive, to fill the void. We allow people to hold us, we get plenty of hugs, and we hold on to a welcoming hand. We find solace writing in our journal. We pray for strength and let God hold our heart in his hands.

What makes a good day? It could be as simple as sunshine pouring in the window. Many of us can accomplish ten times as much on a sunny day. It could be the joy of having a Mass said for our child and feeling their special presence in the Communion of Saints. It could be receiving a loving note from a friend, hearing a piece of music that brings to mind special memories, enjoying the utter devotion of our dog, sipping tea with a friend, reading a book that fills us with inspiration, having supportive colleagues at work, or doing something special in our child's memory. Whatever feels good, include it on your "to do" rescue list and do it again and again. Each of us will have our own list. We just have to remember to use it to turn a bad day into a better day and a good day into one that actually gives us hope.

Dealing with insensitive remarks

The number one complaint of bereaved parents is the insensitive remarks made by well-meaning relatives and friends. Everyone should know that there are no words that will magically take our pain away, but most people feel they must say something to try to comfort us, and many times their words have the reverse effect. The words feel like an arrow piercing our heart or a kick in the stomach taking our breath away. They deplete what little strength we are able to muster. They sap our energy and sometimes paralyze us. They can reduce us to tears and break our fragile spirit.

Some of us find it necessary to avoid people who offer too much unwanted advice. We need time to heal, to process all the words being flung at us. Sometimes we feel like we must run into our cave to avoid more verbal slingshots. It is important for us to feel comfortable, to be able to voice our needs, and to choose words to answer others that will help our healing.

When we are struggling with the death of our child, it doesn't help us to hear pat phrases like: *I know how you feel—my dog died recently. God needed another angel. Your child is in a better place. God only takes the best. You can have another child. You have other children. God only gives you as much as you can bear.* Many times words are meant in a positive way, but we hear them negatively. We are so fragile we can't even sort out the message. We just feel cheated, robbed, lost, confused and angry. Hearing insensitive words or advice from people who think they know what we are going through does not lessen our pain; it seems to inflict more.

Basically, we have to discover responses we can use that will give us relief from our pain. In the beginning, just biting someone's head off with a snippy retort might be all we can muster. For example, a coworker asked a colleague a few months after the death of her child, "Why are you still grieving?" The young mother replied curtly, "Because my child is still dead!" Bereaved parents want to find words to educate people who make insensitive remarks, but it takes time. As we get stronger and our anger dissipates, we can frame sentences in a more diplomatic way that says exactly how we feel, educating the non-bereaved.

As we get further along in our grief, we are better able to handle insensitive words. Finding little prayers or sayings that are like a tonic to our spirit and repeating them again and again to ourselves builds up our immunity to hurtful words. We have to be our own cheerleaders! Humor helps. Here's one prayer that can bring smiles to many of us and help reduce the pain of insensitive words: "Please, Lord, it's my turn for a good day today, isn't it? Maybe tomorrow? Next Tuesday or Wednesday? Half-a-day Thursday? 8:30 to 9:15 Friday morning?"

A light bulb went off in my head one day when I was in church at Easter time a couple of years after Peggy and Denis died. As the priest read Christ's words, "Father, forgive them for they know not what they do," I thought to myself, *What a perfect prayer to say for people who make insensitive remarks to us.* Then I added two words to drive the message home. At our next support group meeting I shared my new prayer with the group and received enthusiastic applause, genuine smiles and spontaneous laughter. I suggested they utter this empowering sentence (to themselves) every time someone said hurtful words to them: "Father, forgive them for they know not what they do, the assholes, Amen." (Now, profanity is not the language I usually use or recommend, but this little addition to Jesus' prayer seems so perfect for this situation that is so demoralizing for us bereaved parents. It allows us to feel in control rather than like a victim stung by insensitive words, even while we are forgiving others for their insensitivity. The amended prayer almost makes us feel sorry for the people making the remarks, rather than being irritated and angry with them. It enables us to keep our dignity instead of being overpowered by hurtful words.)

As the priest read Christ's words, "Father, forgive them for they know not what they do," I thought to myself, What a perfect prayer to say for people who make insensitive remarks to us.

This slightly naughty prayer gets the most reaction of all my remarks at any lecture I give for the bereaved, and the audience is quick to grab pens and jot it down. It is a great piece of humorous armor for grieving parents, answering a vital need for a simple way to ignore the crippling pain caused by the insensitivity of well-meaning friends and relatives.

Surrounding ourselves with loving people who make us

feel comfortable, finding inspiring phrases that talk to our hearts, giving ourselves time and space to figure out our needs, and discovering the right words to educate others will help lessen the sting of insensitive remarks. It might even help eliminate such phrases from the mouths of would-be comforters (but don't count on it).

Giving anger a positive voice

There are no shortcuts through grief. We bereaved parents learn grieving is hard work and that we can't delegate it. Anger, in some form, is connected to our grief. It's the emotion we hide when we tell others, "I'm fine." It is often the most difficult emotion for us to express or even acknowledge, yet it is a normal and healthy response to the death of our child. On the other hand, anger can be all-consuming, monopolizing our daily thoughts and actions. Feelings of anger and hostility can be so overwhelming that we can become stuck in our grief, unable to adequately mourn our loss.

It is important for us to identify and put into words what we are experiencing, as painful as that may be.

The good news is that anger tells us we are alive; the bad news is that we have been programmed to believe nice people don't get angry. It is important for us to identify and put into words what we are experiencing, as painful as that may be. Then we can deal with the feeling, rather than stuffing it deep inside of us, which often creates chronic headaches, stomachaches, back problems, sinus trouble, acne, ulcers, colitis or high blood pressure. Anger needs to be addressed, not denied, so that it does not emerge later in another, more destructive form. Anger, like a caged animal, needs to be set free, which diminishes its power over us.

When our child dies, we can be angry at so many people and for so many things. We want to accuse everyone and everything, and we pass blame around like a hot potato. What we need to do is identify the exact source of our anger. Whom or what are we angry at? Is someone actually to blame for our child's death? We don't want our anger to spill out against innocent targets among our family, friends, neighbors or co-workers, or let bitterness rob us of having a meaningful life again. We have to pinpoint the root of our anger.

We might be angry at ourselves for not preventing the death of our child. As parents, we feel our job is to protect our children. We question ourselves: Did we get to the doctor quickly enough? Did we choose the right doctor? Did we understand the diagnosis and the medication? Did we make intelligent treatment decisions? (In my case with Denis, what did Joe and I know about brain surgery or the surgeon on call? Should we have insisted on having Denis airlifted to a better trauma center? Who can think of all these things in the middle of a life-and-death crisis?)

Perhaps we can't forgive ourselves for giving our child the car keys, for not recognizing early symptoms of illness, for not practicing "tough love" with drugs and alcohol, for giving permission to go on that ski trip, school outing or overnight, or for not stopping them from going swimming, boating, hiking or bicycling. Very possibly we're angry about harsh words that may have been said before the tragedy or other "unfinished business"—especially the "I love yous" that might not have been spoken as often or as clearly as we now wish. Maybe we're just angry at ourselves for not having been a better parent. The result of all this anger is that we do a job on our heads, blaming ourselves for all that has happened, which only keeps feeding our anger.

God might be the target of our anger as well. We rant and rave and ask: *Where were you? Why didn't you prevent this death? Why me? Why my child? Where were you when I needed you?* Even though we vent our anger at God, however, we are really angry with reality itself. In our more rational moments, we know that the loving Father whom Jesus described loves all his children. God did not "take" our child. It is more complex and mysterious than that. Still, it is OK to be angry with God; he can take it!

We might aim our anger at intact families or the world at

large, as we watch others go merrily about their everyday business while we are left stumbling and collapsing. Anger can cause us to delete many names from our address book. It can set up many walls that we will need to dismantle later.

We might focus our anger at others involved in the death of our child: the doctor, the hospital, the ambulance crew, the police, the drunk driver, the drug dealer, the circle of friends, the funeral home, the school, the clergy, or the folks who were not there for us when we needed them. We might be angry at our spouse for grieving differently than we do or not understanding or respecting our way of grieving.

Finally—and this is the absolutely worst part—we might even be angry at our deceased child for leaving us, for hanging out with the wrong friends, for making a poor decision, for driving too fast, for being a daredevil, for being in the wrong spot at the wrong time, for being careless, or for just plain dying on us.

So many issues trigger our anger that sometimes it is hard to sort out the feelings to find the main cause. Sometimes our anger unleashes rage over a traumatic event from the past that we never worked through emotionally, such as a previous death, a divorce, or the loss of a job. That's why our journal writing can help us see the things that set us off. Reading our journal, we can probably decipher a pattern that identifies what causes our anger so we can deal with it appropriately.

We can feel less helpless when we begin to deal with our anger, as anger gives us something to do. We just have to channel it in the right direction, giving it a positive voice. For example, I was angry at the rainy night, the open drawbridge, the poor lighting where the accident that killed my children occurred. Because of my anger and subsequent investigation, there is now a whole new lighting system at the bridge. Every time I drive over the bridge, I say to myself, "Who could believe that one tiny bridge could change my whole life?" Once we recognize our anger, we can express it and eventually let it go, rather than ignoring it and becoming a walking time bomb.

Anger releases pent-up feelings. It responds to physical action such as jogging, racquetball, baseball, tennis, karate, aerobics, bike riding, beating rugs, scrubbing floors, vacuuming, spring cleaning, pounding nails, whitewater rafting and chopping wood. We can scream and yell while we are doing these things, and we can imagine the object of our anger at the other end of our blows.

Crying, sobbing, deep breathing, meditation, thinking about our child being in a better place, talking and writing in our journal all help us process our anger. When we have done a good job depleting our rage, we can better focus on positive steps to redirect the power anger has. We might channel our energy to start a support group, or to volunteer at a chapter of The Compassionate Friends, a Ronald McDonald House, a hospital or a nursing home. We could work with Boy Scouts or Girls Scouts, teach religious education classes, aid Cancer Care, Mothers Against Drunk Driving, or a group that raises money for an illness such as leukemia or heart disease, or work with troubled youth, drug programs, Birthright, blood drives, libraries or church groups. Good things can spring from our terrible loss.

We can find healing in our rage, because acknowledging our anger is a first step toward positive change.

To help diminish our anger, we can write letters to share our feelings with people who added to our anger in some way, even if they didn't mean to. We can then send the letters or rip them up—whatever answers the rage we feel. We can talk to an empty chair, unburdening the weighty problems of our heart, expressing the anger that grips us and feeling the relief of releasing such overwhelming emotions. We can send relatives and friends articles that say so perfectly what is on our mind, attempting to educate them on what we feel and need. We can keep writing in our journal, talking to friends who make no demands on us, and discovering tips on grief suggested in books and magazines by those who have walked before us. These are all concrete ways to deal with our anger. Anger can catapult us into decisive action. We can find healing in our rage, because acknowledging our anger is a first step toward positive change.

Wearing out guilt

Guilt is another tormenting part of grief for us bereaved parents. There are no clear-cut answers to the question of how to relieve it. There are no shortcuts through it, no easy way out. Children always die from a cause, not from old age—even if it is a "natural" cause, such as a terminal disease or birth defect. Since as their parents and protectors we could not prevent their death, we feel responsible. Naturally, we are filled with guilt.

We torture ourselves with unanswerable questions: *Could I have prevented it? Is it my fault? What did I do wrong? How did I fail? Why did I make that decision?* (Denis and Peggy went out on a rainy, foggy evening. Why didn't I insist they change their plans? Why didn't I suggest they do something else that night?) Our guilt feelings are normal, though many times not realistic. The "if onlys" haunt our thoughts day and night. Our mind plays tricks on us as we mentally try to undo what has happened. How we wish we could work miracles and go back and change or prevent the situation that led to our child's death.

> *We're sorry for things we said or did, or didn't say or didn't do.*

We regret lost opportunities—graduations, career choices, weddings, grandchildren. Why didn't we take that trip to Disney World? Why didn't we let her buy that expensive prom dress that made her look like a princess? Who would have been the lucky one he or she married? How successful would he or she have been in a career?

We're sorry for things we said or did, or didn't say or didn't do. Why didn't we make up after that last argument? Why were we so adamant over what time to come home? Phrases like "You're grounded," "Go to your room" and "No telephone" haunt us. We wish we could make up for past mistakes, such as being too strict or not strict enough, teasing about academic or athletic ability, or comparing one child to another. We regret all the things we neglected to do—not being home or involved in their activities enough, for example, or not carving out special time for them in our busy schedule. The list could go on and on because we feel cheated and robbed because we will never see the results of sacrifices we made for them—like the hours spent with school projects, sports teams, church activities, music lessons, and trips to the library. We are filled with remorse that we will never see all our hopes and dreams for our child realized, that there won't be a beautiful ending to the story of their precious life.

We are only human as we heap guilt on ourselves. But why keep blaming ourselves for things that are clearly not our fault? It is healthier for us to think we did the best we could, instead of continually beating ourselves up. Guilt is not satisfied with explanations, and there are none anyway. We need to be honest about why we feel guilty. Then it is important that we talk about it—to a good friend or a trusted counselor, or in the privacy of our journal. Understanding that life is a balance of good and bad, we can begin to accept our imperfections and realize that we can't control what happens in life.

One thing is sure: Our child would not want us to be guilt-ridden for the rest of our life. That thought alone might encourage us to overcome such feelings. Our son or daughter would want us to smile and laugh, to continue living, to enjoy life. We know this deep down in our heart. So we "tell our head" to concentrate on the good times, and we convince ourselves we did the best we could under the circumstances. Our "best" may have varied from day to day depending on life's other pressures and involvements, but contrary to what some bereaved parents think a child's death is not a punishment for something they did (or did not do) in the past.

Try to wear out your guilt, little by little. It does lessen with effort and time. Accept it, understand it, and deal with it. Hold on to *hope* as you ride the roller coaster of grief.

Enjoying permission to be crazy

This was my favorite part of the grief books I read—discovering that I had permission to "be crazy." How wonderful for us grieving parents to be allowed to do anything that gives our heart a moment's peace or joy, as absurd as it may seem, as long as we are not hurting anyone. People who are not bereaved might not understand our actions, but those who are grieving understand perfectly. It's the *crazy* things we dream up to do that bring smiles to our faces, some joy to our hearts, and make us feel *alive* again. So what if others don't understand?

We find different ways to soothe our grief. Collecting angels and adorning my home with these heavenly creatures in every nook and cranny brought me comfort, made me smile, and kept me busy in the early months after my children died. Similarly, many bereaved parents choose other cheerful symbols that remind them of their missing child, such as butterflies, rainbows, unicorns, smiley faces and Disney characters. It might seem crazy to fill a home with sentimental sun-catchers, candles, linens, throws, doormats and ceramic figures, but surrounding ourselves with these meaningful objects can bring a sense of hope and peace by linking us with our child.

Stocking a bathroom with butterfly towels, soap, rugs and curtains or wearing butterfly sweaters, shirts and dresses might add a glow to our day and a bounce to our step. Writing on butterfly stationery or sealing our envelopes with butterfly stickers might bring a special delight. Some parents continue to use their child's name on cards, letters and e-mails, signing their name and adding a phrase like "Ronnie and George and Gary Too from Heaven." It keeps their child included, reminds everyone to always remember him, and does something special for their hearts.

Wearing our children's clothing, enjoying their favorite sweatshirts, sweaters and caps, wrapping ourselves in their snuggly bathrobes and jackets, sporting their favorite pieces of jewelry, listening to their favorite CDs, designing a collection of their framed pictures (some call it a shrine), or lighting all kinds of candles in their memory can create an immediate link with them. One family has kept a tall vigil candle lit continuously since their daughter died, never missing a day, even when they go on vacation. (Neighbors keep the "eternal" flame going.) Another mom carries an 8½ x 11" picture of her daughter wherever she goes—just to feel her presence. On her way to the store she picks up the photo and announces, "Come on, Maryann, we're going shopping." It's amazing what we can find to give our hearts a lift. We have permission to be crazy, and it feels so good!

Bereaved parents deal with their grief in many creative ways. These include sending balloons up to the heavens with loving notes attached; decorating their child's grave with bunny rabbits, pumpkins, red hearts, tiny Christmas trees with lights, stuffed animals and sports paraphernalia; leaving cards and notes at the grave, sprinkling jelly beans there, or simply sitting on the grave reading to their child. One bereaved mother delivered a birthday cupcake complete with lit candle to her daughter's grave—in the pouring rain, no less. Nothing, not even torrential rain, would keep her from celebrating that special day with her daughter. On other days that same mom would join a group of four or five other bereaved mothers. Together they would visit each of their children's graves in different cemeteries spanning 50 miles, adorn them with

> *Some of us set a place at the table, some talk to an empty chair— saying all the things we didn't get to say or just didn't say while our child was alive.*

seasonal decorations, and then go out to lunch. It was a perfect day in their eyes—the beginning of being social again, yet tied directly to their grief.

Some of us set a place at the table, some talk to an empty chair—saying all the things we didn't get to say or just didn't say while our child was alive. Most of us cry our eyes out driving to and from work or while doing our daily errands; we find our car a place of great comfort and privacy, even if the people in the next lane are scratching their heads as they get a glimpse of us. Many of us seek the solace of the shower or the remoteness of a deserted beach to scream our lungs out, away from the eyes of our bereaved family or next-door neighbors. Some of us walk, hike, climb mountains, or enter marathons to exhaust the excruciating pain we feel. Some discover the healing powers of karate as we kick, punch, scream and yell, saving our family and friends from being the targets of our anger. Others delight in the collection of cheap garage-sale crockery—so we have ammunition handy to throw at cement walls, feeling the exhilaration of breaking the dishes and ridding ourselves of pent-up rage. Yes, creating our own "wailing wall" allows us to empty ourselves of some of the anguish that consumes us. Crazy, huh?

Some of us write about all the issues we are angry about or simply pen letters asking forgiveness for certain actions or misunderstandings. And then we burn them, symbolically ridding ourselves of all the hurtful feelings they represent. Keeping our child very much in mind, we learn to find ways to include him or her in all the things we do. I always put my children in charge of the weather for major events such as weddings and big parties, and they have a marvelous track record in getting us sunny skies for these occasions. Their success rate is so high that I get calls from friends all over the United States requesting Peggy's and Denis' help, which definitely makes my heart sing!

Keeping our child very much in mind, we learn to find ways to include him or her in all the things we do.

One family chose a simple pink rose to put across a plate at their son's wedding, reminding them their daughter was with them in spirit for that special day. Others put framed pictures on or near the altar at the weddings of their remaining children as a way to include their deceased child in the festivities. The non-bereaved may make faces or roll their eyes at some of these choices, but they have no idea how much these loving rituals help us bereaved parents get through a special occasion standing up. (At my daughter Annie's wedding, a special votive candle in memory of Peggy and Denis was brought up at the Presentation of Gifts and placed on the altar. It was sparkling and it glowed just like Tinkerbell, seeming to say, "We're here with you!")

Like me, many bereaved parents ask their child's help in the mundane routines of daily life. It could be a favorite plea—Peggy and Denis are excellent at finding me parking spaces—or others, like matching socks, balancing a checkbook, getting a stain out, or prompting traffic to move faster. It feels good to think our children are interceding for us, whether it's a coincidence or not. And it feels good to talk to them about the little problems that cause potholes and hurdles for us on our journey. We find it comforting to seek our child's help, as weird as it may seem to others.

Some families are doing things that were never even thought of years ago, such as painting their child's casket a favorite color or choosing a casket now available in decorator colors with a choice of popular graphics—Disney characters, sports emblems, school logos and such. They ignore tradition and bury their child in a sports uniform, dance recital costume, favorite outfit of sweatshirt and jeans, comfy bunny slippers, or whatever was special to that child. Favorite stuffed animals, CDs, yearbooks, newspapers, sports caps, musical instruments or other personal items are lovingly tucked into the casket. One father wrapped his teenage daughter in his "lucky" blanket, which had gone through the hell of Vietnam with him. It had kept him safe, and he wanted his daughter to be kept safe on her heavenly journey. Denis' father (we were divorced) took Denis' lifeguard whistle off the top of the closed casket and shocked everybody by blowing it out loud as relatives and friends filed out of the funeral home on the way to the church services. It broke the grief-filled tension and replaced tears with smiles. It was a reminder of Denis' love of the ocean and years of surfing and touched a special chord in everybody's heart.

We all do what helps our heart deal with this terrible loss. Permission to be crazy offers many avenues of comfort to bereaved parents. Make sure you use that permission to find some ways to ease the burden in your heart.

---

*Then you shall call, and the Lord will answer;
you shall cry for help, and he will say, Here I am.*
Isaiah 58:9

Finding Our Way Through the Power of Words

Then they cried to the Lord in their trouble,
and he saved them from their distress;
he sent his word and healed them,
and delivered them from destruction.

Psalm 107:19-20

Discovering books as a lifeline

All I wanted to know after the deaths of my children was how I could possibly go on living: *Is there a school for bereaved parents? Is there a number you call? Where do I turn? When will this nightmare end?*

Frantic for answers, I read everything I could get my hands on regarding grief. I devoured every book the public library had on the subject. Then I haunted the bookstores. I searched their shelves for words that would soothe my mind and ease my pain. Filling myself with heartfelt poetry and prose written by people who had been bereaved before me, I found guidelines for surviving. Story after story touched my heart and gave me hope. I discovered that people actually survived the death of their child.

Books were my lifeline. They validated my feelings and offered me some choices of things to do to survive. I found positive thoughts and strategies to try. Hope jumped off the pages, renewing my spirit. Phrases stuck in my mind, replaying insightful bits of information. I found helpful resources such as addresses and phone numbers listed for organizations, support groups and magazines, most of which I had never known existed.

Books make wonderful gifts to ourselves and to those who

want to understand our pain. We can invite books to talk to us when we want their company, and we can close their covers when we don't. We can smile, cry or even rage as we read them, and they will never tell. They make no demands and never put us on a timetable. They can bring much comfort and offer coping suggestions that would never have crossed our minds. They can fill us with good ideas, especially for tough days. They can validate our feelings, assuring us we are not going crazy. Books can give us energy to try new coping strategies, renewing our will to live.

Journaling is one of the best ways to heal the painful feelings of loss.

Books can be like a life preserver, keeping us afloat when we feel as if we are drowning.

Books last long after the flowers have withered, the casseroles have been eaten, and the sympathy cards have been packed away. They whisper to our inner voice and answer some of the questions of our heart. They can bring a moment's peace and inspire music in a sorrowful spirit. They can release the vise that seems to grip our heart. They can be wise friends sharing their wisdom with us, in our own space, on our own time.

Recording the heart's voice

Even while our heart is breaking, many issues still consume our energy and add to our distress. Naming our feelings and dealing with them helps us get back some control of our life and process the issues tangled in our grief.

Journaling is one of the best ways to heal the painful feelings of loss. Recording our feelings daily or just writing a few sentences sporadically enables us to see what we are feeling, whether it be anger, guilt, loneliness, frustration, low self-esteem, worry, fear, sadness, confusion, depression, or any other feeling that engulfs us. Journaling allows us to let off steam, to unload burdens, to release pent-up feelings that need to be expressed. We discover what we are thinking and how we are feeling. We get in touch with our true selves. Feelings are neither right nor wrong; naming them and claiming them dissipates the negative power they have on us and opens our hearts to positive ideas.

Not only does writing in a journal help us process our grief, it records our day-by-day journey so that we can actually see the things that make us tick. We can follow our heart's progress. We discover what gives us a boost and what knocks us down. We recognize the people who give us comfort and the ones we should keep at arm's length. We find the places that ease our pain and the settings to avoid. Just by reading what we have written, we discover mood swings, living patterns, the love of special friends, the undeniable comfort of a family pet. If we've written about how something in a book helped us, or how a song we heard affected us, or how a place of scenic beauty nourished our spirit, it allows us to realize the healing power of books, music and nature.

No one told me back then about journaling. One of my biggest regrets is that I did not keep a journal early on in my grieving. How I would love to know now what I was thinking and feeling in those early days of sorrow. Instead, I fell into bed every night and was asleep as my head hit the pillow, never affording myself the few minutes it would have taken to jot down my feelings from the day. I missed a great opportunity to record the depth and path of my sorrow.

How healing it is to note your progress and see your growth as you page back in your journal, shaking your head, not believing the thoughts you had and the feelings you experienced. How wonderful it is to note what helped you so you can repeat it again and again on tough days. How informative it is to be aware of situations you handled well and those you must steer clear of until you are a little stronger. A journal is like a road map, pointing us in the right direction and offering us various avenues on our grief journey.

All we have to do is write honestly, from the heart, whenever we wish. Of course, it helps to set aside a special time on a regular basis in a comfy spot where we can get in touch with our feelings. The ritual can offer us a quiet time to release all the daily frustrations and sadness that envelop us and also can provide a time to explore the occasional joys that slide in and out of our daily life. We can write in a simple notebook or treat ourselves to one of the beautiful journals offered in bookstores and card shops. Or we might prefer to use our computer and file the heartfelt printouts in a binder. (An especially good journaling book, *The New Day Journal,* designed by my friend and colleague Sr. Mauryeen O'Brien is aimed specifically at those grieving the loss of a loved one.)

What to write? Besides recording our daily ups and downs, we might find it helpful to write a letter to our dead child. It could be an opportunity to say goodbye if we never had that chance. It could be another way to remind our child of the love we have for him or her, or just to say "I love you" once again. It might provide an avenue for discussing unfinished business, or for expressing anger or guilt. It might just be to stay in touch, telling what our daily life is like right now, or it could be begging for forgiveness for something we feel terrible about. It might just express gratitude for the years of joy our child brought into our life, or simply for the years we shared.

In our journals we might like to write a letter to ourselves, pretending it is our dead child writing to us, imagining what he or she would like to say to us if there were a chance. We could write a letter to our spouse, to our other children, to relatives and friends, or even to other bereaved parents, explaining how we feel. (We might even give them a copy if it is appropriate to spell out our innermost thoughts to them.) We also could write a letter to God, expressing our deep gratitude to him for our precious child or our overwhelming anger at him for letting our child die. (Either way, God will still love us.)

We can use our journals to describe all the things we remember about our child—physical description, virtues and faults, triumphs and disappointments, special occasions enjoyed together, memorable trips, favorite sayings, and whatever sports, hobbies and interests delighted our child. We can write our child's biography, including basic facts and all our dreams and desires, highlighting what was so special about him or her and retelling the circumstances of the death. We can write poetry and prose about our child or about our broken hearts.

Keeping a journal is an important step for bereaved parents. By journaling we can record and replay the roller coaster of feelings that humbles us each day—and learn grief's great lessons.

Empowering spirits

How our day can change when we are uplifted and energized by the words of a timely phone call, the message of a printed card or handwritten note, or the lyrics of a beautiful song. How many ways there are to touch our aching hearts with soothing words. How wonderful it is to feel empowered by something as simple as words.

After the funeral or memorial service is over and all our caretakers have left us alone to resume our life, feelings of loneliness and depression often can overwhelm us. That's the time when we most appreciate a loving phone call to bolster our spirits. Just a friendly "hello" or a thoughtful "I was thinking of you" can help lift us out of the doldrums. Knowing people care about us is the best tonic for our fragile being. The phone calls don't have to be long, for there are no words to "fix" our grief. They just let us know someone cares.

Knowing people remember our loved one in a special way helps our hearts.

Sometimes we don't feel like talking or answering the phone, but someone leaving a message can communicate caring to us, and that's what's important—that we know someone is thinking of our child, and of us.

Some people are afraid to call us for fear they will say the wrong thing or because they don't know exactly what to say, so they take the safe path and send a warm card or note to cheer us. Stores today offer a great variety of greeting cards of encouragement—some can even make us smile in our grief. Knowing people remember our loved one in a special way helps our hearts. Inspiring words can motivate us to take a tiny step forward in our grief. After the initial flood of sympathy cards has diminished, a simple friendship card can renew our determination to keep taking those baby steps to recovery. Handwritten notes with loving thoughts and prayers can add a happy moment to our day. We can read and reread the warm phrases again and again to empower us to keep going.

One woman whose son was a lifeguard with my son and whom I had never met before the accident sent me a personal note every month reminding me how special my children were—and she had never met *them* either. But she was a mother with children the age of mine, and she could not imagine losing two at one time. She did what she could do best—write from her heart. She never missed a holiday, anniversary or birthday, and she continues to this day. Her notes and cards continue to bring tears to my eyes and a lump to my throat. Over the years she has been my cheerleader, urging me to keep going no matter how many obstacles were in my path. Our families became inseparable after meeting a year later—a blessing and a gift that resulted directly from her heartfelt words.

> *Certain songs have the marvelous ability to recall happy occasions or specific events in our child's life that help us to savor precious memories.*

For some of us, music can soothe our aching souls, whether it be classical, instrumental, spiritual, rock and roll, country, or show tunes. Melodies can lull us into a relaxed state, giving us a few minutes of peace, a time for guided imagery, or perhaps a soothing background for journaling. Certain songs have the marvelous ability to recall happy occasions or specific events in our child's life that help us to savor precious memories. But it's the lyrics of many songs that whisper to our hearts with just the right words to give us a sense of comfort or to make us feel a special connection with our child. When we find a song that lifts our spirits we usually play it over and over, sometimes wearing out the tape or CD, just like I did with a beautiful tape of religious songs called "Celebrate." My husband never complained as I dusted and vacuumed and sang my heart out to the tunes that spoke so strongly to me. He might have felt like smashing the boom box, but he never said a word as he listened to me sing along, and believe me I am no Celine Dion! Words can be a powerful tool in creating our "new normal," giving us inspiration and easing our pain. You just have to find the right ones.

Grasping the message of support groups

There is a solace in being with others who have suffered the death of a child, knowing we are not alone and realizing there are people with whom we can share our fears and tears. Finding a support group where we feel comfortable and safe to talk about our child is another big step for us bereaved parents. Although general bereavement groups often welcome us, it is very helpful if we can find one for parents who have lost a child, one that offers us strategies and relationships for coping with that unique loss.

Every grief book I read mentioned The Compassionate Friends, a national organization for bereaved parents (and siblings) with almost 600 chapters across the United States. I had never heard of the group before my children died. Since there were no chapters in our area, I asked my husband if together we could start one in our hometown so we could benefit from all the wonderful things I had read about the organization. Joe and I applied for a charter from the national office in Oak Brook, Illinois, found three other bereaved parents as the required core group, did the paperwork and publicity, and opened the doors to our chapter of The Compassionate Friends fifteen months after burying Peggy and Denis. We guessed 10 to 15 people would show up for our monthly meetings at the local college. To our surprise, we had 36 bereaved parents at our first meeting, filling up every chair in the classroom. Every month thereafter we had to move to a bigger room to accommodate the ever-growing crowd—sometimes more than 100 people. We had no idea there were so many bereaved parents out there. And like us, they needed the support of people who understood the unique pain of losing a child.

We listened to tapes purchased from the national office, and each month I led the discussion afterward. Even though I was an educator by profession, it was truly an example of the blind leading the blind, because I was as newly bereaved as the rest of the group. But we learned so much from the recorded messages and from the sharing that followed. Our meetings were lively and invigorating, using topics the parents craved, such as dealing with anger, fighting guilt and relating to our spouse. Founded in 1987, our chapter continues to grow, with four or five new families joining us each month.

Being in a safe place with others who are grieving allows us bereaved parents time to share our feelings, talk about our child, tell our story, and learn something about the grief process. If only we could take "before" and "after" pictures. People coming to the group for the first time are nervous, agitated, scared and sniffling. They usually leave the first meeting with a feeling of hope, specific suggestions for coping, and many times a lighter step. They return month after month finding what they need in the healing process: a safe place to express their grief, loving listeners, helpful sharing of ideas and feelings, education about the grief process, and special rituals in memory of their child, such as our December candle-lighting ceremonies or plantings in our memorial garden. They continue to go on learning, sharing and getting stronger, often making new friends and reaching out to the newcomers.

A support group provides an environment offering hope and the means for re-energizing our life. It emphasizes and repeats the facts of normal grief reactions, dispels some myths about grief, and encourages the sharing of thoughts and the release of feelings. It offers a forum for haunting questions to be answered. For example, we learn that feelings we thought only we had—such as wanting to die to be with our child—are really quite common. It is a place to find friendship with people who understand our pain and can talk to us about it—not change the subject or tell us what we *should* do, as so many of our well-meaning friends and relatives are wont to do. A support group offers topics to enlighten us, a chance to talk about our child, telephone buddies to call on a rough day, suggestions for coping, books to read, ideas for honoring birthdays and anniversaries, and practice at being around people and telling our story.

Support groups motivate us to try things we never thought of doing to help us through our grief. They show us how to reinvest the special love we have for our child so that it isn't wasted—so that the world remembers our child and therefore something good can come from this great loss. They stir something within us, empowering us to lead a meaningful life again. We help ourselves, we make lifetime friends, we feel alive again—that's a good beginning and wonderful motivation for trying a support group.

At that fragile, frenzied time when we could barely stand, how did we find the time, energy or strength to put into words the thoughts about our child that were monopolizing our mind?

How do you find one? Check with the reference desk at the public library; look in church bulletins, hospital newsletters, calendars of events in local newspapers, sources listed in grief support books, and community pages in the phone book; ask clergy members, other bereaved friends, therapists, social workers, or funeral home directors. Most groups are free. Choose one that feels comfortable to you. Attend a few times to give it a fair chance. If it does not answer your needs, try another one. You will know when you feel like you're *home*: You can grasp the healing message.

Sharing the journey through writing and speaking

Our heart screams to tell the story of our child, and our whole being cries out for the therapeutic release of sharing these thoughts and memories. In the days before the wake and the funeral, many of us wanted to write a special eulogy or design a unique memorial card or program to hand out so that people would remember our child. At that fragile, frenzied time when we could barely stand, how did we find the time, energy or strength to put into words the thoughts about our child that were monopolizing our mind? I think the Holy Spirit was watching over us.

All I knew was I wanted the world to know how much I loved my daughter and how special she was. (Four days later I wanted the same for my son). I can remember waking up at three o'clock in the morning, sitting in the kitchen and pouring my heart out on paper, scribbling the eulogy for her funeral Mass. I had no trouble finding the right words; they just flowed along with the tears. Then I prayed for the strength to deliver the eulogy myself. (I did ask my dearest friend, who also happened to be Peggy's godmother, to accompany me to the pulpit in case I couldn't voice the loving words I had prepared.) When I approached the altar a wave of emotion washed over everyone in the cathedral. Everyone seemed to sense my pain, but I did make it through. That was the beginning of my writing about my children. I still call it "sharing Peggy and Denis with the world."

When I approached the altar a wave of emotion washed over everyone in the cathedral.

Six weeks later, when I had gotten a little stronger, I pondered what kind of acknowledgement card I could send to thank everyone for their generous support—notes and cards, dedicated Masses and prayers, flowers and plants, memorial vestments and vessels, food trays and errands. I even visited a local printing firm to steal some ideas, but I found none expressing what my heart wanted to say. So I turned to designing and writing my own card, which folded like a birthday card. On the front I composed my heartfelt "thank you" for all the wonderful things that had been done for us. It appeared under a favorite childhood picture of Peggy and Denis, "the inseparable duo." Inside the card I told everybody the special things I remembered about my Peggy and Denis, with Peggy's picture and story on the left side and Denis' picture and story on the right. Information about the memorial scholarship established in their names was on the back of the card. To this day I share the writings on that card with people I meet so they will know my children. No one could have told me how one piece of writing, composed in those early days of grief, could help my heart so much and for so long!

I also asked relatives and friends to share stories of my children and compiled these tales into a little booklet, gifting special people with a copy. Then I began to write more and more about my experience as a bereaved parent, and I found that sharing what helped me cope with my children's deaths was very healing for me. Reaching out to other bereaved families with the simple wisdom I had learned in my months of grieving brought joy to my tears.

The more I learned about grieving, the more I wrote to help other families know they could survive. The articles I wrote for newspapers, magazines and newsletters led to groups for bereaved people inviting me to speak to their members. Then I was invited to speak at national bereavement conferences and seminars across the United States. Never did I dream that my words could help so many people and that so many people would remember my children—Peggy and Denis were not to be erased after all! As one bereaved mother wrote to me recently, "Isn't it wonderful that even after all these years Peggy and Denis still make a difference in the world?" And I thought, *Oh God, the power of words makes my heart sing!*

Many other bereaved parents find the strength to share their thoughts in public, empowering bereaved audiences to deal positively with their grief and educating those who want to know how to help the bereaved. Whether lecturing for Mothers Against Drunk Driving, Cancer Care, Survivors of Suicide, drug rehabilitation programs, Parents of Murdered Children or any other special group, most of these grieving parents find they are doing something they never dreamed they could do—getting up and speaking in front of a group. But they do it with determination, love and pride, knowing they are doing it in memory of their child. One mom I met now shares her heartfelt story of burying all four of her children: a 2-year-old son who died of leukemia in 1979, and her 14-year-old son and 10-year-old daughter, who were shot and killed years later by their 23-year-old brother, who then shot and killed himself and seriously wounded his father (he missed his mother), all because of drug addiction. She wants families to understand the heartache drugs can bring, so she tells her story. You can bet that every audience sits up and listens to her message.

The grief journey will bring many surprises and many gifts. We have no idea what lies ahead. We can't even dream of the obstacles we will encounter, the mountains we will climb, the valleys we will stumble through, or the soothing waters that will revive our spirit. Even though there are no words to magically bring back our child or to adequately describe our pain, the power of words may open the door to many blessings.

How sweet are your words to my taste,
sweeter than honey to my mouth!

Psalm 119:103

Struggling with Special Issues

Relieve the troubles of my heart,
and bring me out of my distress.

Psalm 25:17

Enduring sudden death

When the death of a child comes without any warning, and it often does, it adds more tasks to the complex work of our grieving. The brutal shock of the news is so overwhelming and so painful that we can be immobilized for a time, both physically and psychologically, unable to get our bearings. The mind mercifully shuts down and numbness sets in, giving us time to regroup to deal with the facts. Our responses are involuntary, beyond our control. We are overwhelmed, and our coping capacity is severely diminished. We don't get time to prepare or to gradually absorb the reality. We must cope with something that has already happened.

Shock slows everything down. We can't just "snap out of it." It takes time to come to grips with the situation; our responses vary. Some of us can't stand or speak or think. Some retreat to our beds. Others rant and rave, throw things, run from the scene, or pound the nearest object or person. These are all ways of distancing ourselves from the reality, with which we simply don't know how to deal. The world we know has been changed forever, and our minds and hearts don't want to accept that fact. We may have to go over the story many times while attempting to make sense of the loss, and we may feel totally exhausted dealing with such an unexpected assault on our minds and bodies.

After receiving the call that my son had been injured in an automobile accident, my husband and I rushed to the hospital, but we were assuming it was nothing more serious than a broken arm or leg. Since nobody had mentioned Peggy being with Denis, even though they had gone to the beach concert together, we assumed they had gone different ways after the concert, as kids do.

We got to spend a few minutes with our unconscious son as they prepared him for brain surgery. When I asked about Peggy the doctor told me she was at the scene of the accident.

My whole world collapsed in an instant.

I immediately thought, *Good ol' Peggy, why didn't she get in the ambulance with Denis instead of minding his pride-and-joy car?* The startled doctor looked at me and said: "You don't understand. Your daughter didn't make it. She died at the scene." It was as if a lightning bolt had hit me. My whole world collapsed in an instant.

Within minutes of the news about Peggy we watched a priest give Denis the Last Rites, which is now called the sacrament of the Anointing of the Sick. I gently kissed him before they whisked him off to the operating room. While Denis was in surgery, Joe and I drove home to tell Annie what had happened. (She had stayed home to tell Peggy what had happened.) I kept thinking: *Where do you get the words to tell your daughter that the sister who has always been her roommate is dead and that her big brother is fighting for his life?* I remember Annie just stared at us in utter disbelief, as if we were speaking a foreign language she had never heard before.

After getting a friend to come and stay with Annie, Joe and I drove to the county morgue a few minutes away. We identified our beautiful Peggy lying behind the glass viewing wall of the morgue, and then almost immediately began running between the funeral parlor and the intensive care unit to spend precious time with our two children, one now dead and the other hanging on to life by the thinnest of threads. Annie joined us on our dual vigil.

For two days, relatives and close friends sat by Denis' bedside in the intensive care unit, talking to him and playing music for him, hoping to get him to open his eyes, while Annie, Joe and I greeted people at the funeral home. We would visit Denis at odd hours of the day and night. The nurses looked the other way, respecting our unfathomable tragedy.

Denis died the day after we buried Peggy, never regaining consciousness. How did we plan two funerals in one week? I can only report that the Lord gave us special strength to get through all the rituals. In fact I am sure he was carrying us, as is described so beautifully in the popular poem "Footprints." Shock numbed us to the scope of our loss as we robotically dealt with all the details of wakes, funerals, organ donation, police investigation and media. It wasn't until all our caretakers left the evening of the second funeral and Joe, Annie and I were left alone that we looked at each other in disbelief, thinking: *How do we keep going? How do we pick up the pieces and reinvent our life? How can we continue to live in this too quiet house?* We had no answers—just endless questions.

As shock begins to fade, denial comes to the rescue. It is so tempting for us bereaved parents to believe that it's all been a horrible mistake, that someone is lying, that the phone will ring, that the door will open, that we will hear that special voice again. I could console myself by imagining that my children were still away at college, that they were visiting friends, or that they were enjoying a much-anticipated vacation and I was simply awaiting their return. Denial gives us a temporary respite to gather our strength to face the awful work of grieving to come. It is like a protective cushion shielding our hearts and minds from a fact too horrible to face. But eventually it crumbles and we are brought face to face with the terrible truth that our child has died.

What haunts a lot of us dealing with a sudden death is the fact that we did not get a chance to prepare for the death, to say goodbye, to say a final "I love you," to clarify some misunderstanding, to square away some unfinished business, or just to fully enjoy for one last time the wonders of our child. Sudden death freezes the parent-child relationship in time. Dwelling on these lost opportunities adds to the torture of imagining our child's pain and aloneness at the time of death. Regret over things we didn't say or do also can torment us. We can still say them or write about them, but our hearts wish we had been able to express these feelings while our child was alive. Here is our choice: We can continually blame ourselves and give ourselves a life sentence with no parole, or we can get the facts and realize that we did our best under the circumstances and with the knowledge we had available.

Since many sudden deaths are also violent—car accidents, plane crashes, fires, shootings, stabbings, suicide, terror attacks—we not only have to face the death of our child but also the mutilation of our child's body. As much as we might not want to look upon our dead child, seeing the body makes the death real for us. Visiting the scene; gathering the facts; reclaiming personal effects; and talking to emergency personnel, hospital staff, or the police who worked the case all help us know what happened. One bereaved mother made a date for lunch with the medical examiner because she had to understand the autopsy findings. The sensitive M.E. consoled her by helping make the death real to her. The mom needed the facts to process her grief and to shed the safety net of denial.

If a child died suddenly from a medical cause, such as a heart attack or heart condition, aneurysm, SIDS, asthma attack, undiagnosed fatal disease, failed operation, infection, or genetic disorder unknown to us, we tend to blame ourselves for not knowing about the condition, or not getting to the doctor fast enough, or even for not choosing the *right* doctor or hospital. If a household accident or sports trauma caused the death, we reproach ourselves for not being more cautious, not being at the scene to prevent the accident, or not insisting on more safety precautions or better safety equipment. We fill ourselves with "if onlys"—the fantasies that we should have been able to control what happened—which offer us temporary relief from the feeling of helplessness: *If only I had noticed the lump. If only we hadn't gone out to dinner. If only we hadn't given him/her the car keys.*

If someone's negligence, violence or incompetence caused our child's death, we can be filled with a rage that consumes our every thought. The "if onlys" are accompanied by a desire for revenge and speedy justice. (We often find a need for strenuous physical activity to be able to deal with the overwhelming anger in these cases. As one mom said, "Gardening saved my sanity. I worked there until I dropped. My garden was my intensive care unit." Another parent said karate saved his marriage. "I could yell, scream, kick, swing—all the things I wanted to do to that drunk driver, instead of taking it out on my wife.")

Sudden death leaves permanent scars—reminding us we are mortal, that death doesn't always happen to someone else, that we don't know the "day or hour," that this could happen again to someone we love. But it can also prompt us to live each day in a special way, to appreciate life, to deal with unfinished business, to not put things off, to tell our loved ones how much they mean to us, to discover what is important to us, and to establish meaningful priorities.

Our response to the sudden death of our child can be our savior. We can find a positive voice for our anger and devote our energies to ways of having our child remembered, such as establishing scholarships, working with or starting a foundation, sponsoring trips for the disabled, granting wishes of terminally ill children, planting gardens, funding libraries, writing articles, or giving talks to the bereaved. Or we can try to change the conditions that led to our child's death, by working with school sports programs to make them safer, highway commissions to redesign killer roads, or campaigns for hospital reform, better patient care, and zero tolerance of medical error. Everything we do is to help keep our child's memory very much alive. As one parent said: "My child's gone; I'm still here. My job is to figure out my purpose now." My favorite mantra, "If their song is to continue, then we must do the singing," keeps me busy finding many projects to keep my children's memories alive.

As one parent said: "My child's gone; I'm still here. My job is to figure out my purpose now."

Living through extended illness

Parents seem to respond to the death they are dealt. While those enduring sudden death are grateful they didn't have to watch their child suffer, parents living through extended illness are grateful they had the extra time with their child to talk, to say "I love you" as many times as they wished, to do things they wanted to do for their sick child, to complete "unfinished business," to gather friends and family, and to prepare themselves for dealing with the death of their child. They saw their child go downhill, stage by stage, just as the doctors predicted; they had time to process the information and prepare themselves as best they could.

Still, even though a terminal illness has been diagnosed, many of us refuse to give up hope that our child will beat the odds and recover miraculously. We spend hours in the library or on the Internet tracking down new medications, theories, treatments and doctors. We check out every bit of information we can find. With our limited medical knowledge, we pray to make the right decisions regarding the choices offered to us. What a heavy burden it is wondering whether we have made the correct decision, especially when doctors disagree. We encounter additional pain if we disagree with our spouse on what choices to make.

> *It is exhausting being torn in so many directions and trying to give each responsibility a fair amount of time.*

We try to be with our child as much as possible. This causes problems with our work and with other family members, who need and demand our attention too. It is exhausting being torn in so many directions and trying to give each responsibility a fair amount of time. Some of us cut back on work and family obligations, depending on others to do things such as driving on our carpool days, watching our children after school, walking the dog or even doing our birthday or Christmas shopping for us. As the illness progresses, we find ourselves devoting all our energies to our dying child.

As hope diminishes, anticipating the death of our child allows us to seek comfort from family, friends, clergy, therapists and support groups to answer our questions and fears. It gives us time to respond to the wishes of our dying child and to make preliminary funeral arrangements. It also allows us to honor the requests of our child regarding readings, music and participants in the funeral ritual, if he or she is mature enough to discuss and participate in such decisions.

These kinds of conversations among all the family members can be a golden opportunity to do things that not only help us but also help our dying child. They can bring us closer together, smoothing out old hurts, reinforcing the strength and comforts of our faith, and emphasizing the treasures of family stories and memories. The result can make the child's death a more peaceful and grace-filled experience and set the stage for a more positive bereavement experience for everyone concerned.

But even when parents are blessed with precious time to spend with their dying child, their lives change drastically after the funeral. One mother declared: "There is a huge hole in my day! After cutting back on work, family obligations, socializing, vacations, sports, and hobbies—basically ignoring the world—to tend to my child's needs, I now feel life is suddenly very empty. The hospital equipment, the medicines, the routine, the nurses, doctors, therapists—they're all gone. Nothing is the same."

Surviving suicide

Losing a child to suicide compounds the grief of sudden death a thousandfold. Along with the shock and numbness and the questioning eyes of society, we parents have to deal with the gnawing and many times unanswerable question of "Why?" We are haunted by thoughts such as: *What could I have done to prevent it? Why didn't I see it coming? Why couldn't my child ask me for help? How could my child do this to me?*

We feel guilt, shame and anger that almost paralyze us. We suffer a keen sense of failure, knowing we could not save our own child's life. We feel an overwhelming sense of personal rejection, a desertion, a slap in the face, a disregard of all the values we tried to instill. We sense everyone is looking at us, pointing a finger at us, and assuming our family is dysfunctional. We feel humiliation, disapproval, and the fear that this could happen again in our family. The stigma of suicide goes deep and torments our souls, forcing us to question our self-worth, our God, and our life in general.

As hard as it is for us parents to say the word "suicide," it helps us to face the reality. Some find it easier to say that their child "took" his or her own life. Saying it either way helps us deal with the facts that we can piece together about our child's death, to be honest with ourselves, and to be honest with others. People who have survived their own suicide attempts say suicide was not so much a wish to be dead but rather a desperate attempt to end their intense, unrelenting emotional pain. The extreme pain of living with no relief in sight was simply too great for our child.

After the suicide, we review our interactions with our child, talk with our child's friends, teachers, doctors and others who knew our child, and read and reread notes and papers left behind, looking for clues that led to his or her decision. Sometimes the pieces fit together to create a clear picture that offers us an explanation, but other times we cannot be sure whether or not our child intended to kill himself or herself. This uncertainty can add to our already heavy burden of grief and can hinder the healing process.

Even though some parents find it unbearable to say their child died from suicide, studies show that dealing with the facts and being up-front about them helps recovery. Suicide frightens people and makes them feel uncomfortable, causing friends to purposely avoid us. One bereaved mother who lost her daughter to suicide yelled in frustration to her neighbor, "Suicide isn't contagious!" as the neighbor kept crossing the street to avoid talking to her. The isolation, the insensitive actions, the hurtful comments that are expressed or implied—all take their toll as we try to rebound from the trauma of our child's suicide.

Here is simple advice, garnered from many parents I have met or comforted after the suicide of their child: Ignore those who cast aspersions, treasure those who stand by you, and move on to find new sources of support. It helps if you can broach the subject of your child's suicide with others, opening the door for your friends' support and concern. Your willingness to talk about your child's death gives people permission to talk about it and helps remove the stigma of silence that usually surrounds suicide.

Reading everything we can about suicide helps us understand some of the causes and gives us suggestions for coping. In most cases external circumstances—such as the loss of a job, a fight with a loved one or friend, divorce, failure in school, or disobeying parental rules—are not *causes* of suicide but rather *triggers*. Usually the trigger is the last thing a person was upset about, but suicide has its roots in the biology of the brain. The brain is an organ and can get sick like any other organ. When one father had a hard time dealing with the reasons behind his daughter's suicide, his wife gently offered, "Just think of it as cancer of the brain." That allowed him to see the suicide in a different light. A combination of genes, environment, psychological reactions and social factors create the diseases of the brain that we call mental illness. Depression, bipolar disorder and schizophrenia are three mental illnesses caused by brain chemistry imbalances that may result in suicide. A chemical imbalance in the brain is harder to detect than a broken leg or heart disease. Although suicide is not inherited, predispositions to mental illnesses can be inherited, just as they can for heart disease or diabetes. We learn that the treatment for mental illness is medicine, psychotherapy or a combination of both. Finding the right doctor and the right medication are big factors in battling mental illness, but more often than not it goes undiagnosed. Contrary to what most people think, suicide has nothing to do with willpower, how a person was raised, or failure of character. It is a matter of biochemistry and genetics.

> *Contrary to what most people think, suicide has nothing to do with willpower, how a person was raised, or failure of character.*

"I can survive if I choose to" is a mantra that parents of suicide victims can repeat over and over each day. They must surround themselves with loving family and friends who can talk with them, listen to their heartache, and remind them that they are good and decent people. Family and friends can be a safety net, keeping parents from sinking lower than they already feel. Some parents, overwhelmed with shame and humiliation over a suicide, opt for a private funeral with no wake, denying themselves crucial support at a time when it is most needed. Parents of suicide victims need to seek professional help right away, aware that everyone in the family has been injured and needs help to make sense of the loss, to understand what has happened, and to find

Children who are intent on taking their life will often find a way despite our best efforts.

a way to go on. Adjusting to the agonizing loss and the glaring hole in the family fabric will be painful and take time. It's usually one step forward and two steps back. Parents have to keep talking, avoiding the silence that can lead to chronic depression, isolation and the death of spirit. They must learn to hold their heads high, relishing their love for their child, and not allowing anyone to diminish their pride in their child's character.

Lifelong problems may have surrounded your child, but remember, you did your best to help him or her try to surmount them. None of us can be with our child 24 hours a day; children who are intent on taking their life will often find a way despite our best efforts. So continue to read about suicide and find solace in comforting prose and poetry. To further your healing, eat right, exercise in moderation, get rest, meditate, grieve openly, and remind yourself that you are not to blame. Whatever emotions you feel should be expressed. Naming and dealing with the devastation, hopelessness, desolation, sadness, confusion, frustration, shame and whatever else about your child's suicide shatters your equilibrium will help you to overcome the obstacles to resolving your grief and to believe that you will survive and lead a meaningful life again.

Dealing with murder or accidental killing

The death of a child by murder or accidental killing brings

another unique form of parental grief. To know our child has been shot, stabbed, violated, mutilated or tormented in some way inflicts devastating emotional trauma on us that lasts a lifetime. The suddenness, the violence involved, the mental imagery of the crime, the intentional or irrational nature of the act, and our child's lack of choice or warning all combine to shatter our existence and complicate and prolong our grief. Many people, even in our support system, can't deal with the intensity of our mourning in this situation. Becoming uncomfortable, they begin to distance themselves from our pain, leaving us lonely and isolated.

We are overwhelmed with anger, rage, bitterness, guilt, helplessness, terror, bewilderment, frustration, and feelings of revenge. We keep asking ourselves: *Did my child suffer? Was my child filled with fear? Could I have protected my child? Why wasn't I there when my child needed me? How can I get the person who did this to my child?* We are filled with "if onlys": *If only I had driven my daughter there instead of letting her walk. If only I had insisted on an earlier time for him to be home. If only I had warned my child more about talking to strangers. If only I had put my foot down about the crowd he was hanging out with.* We feel terribly guilty about not having been able to protect our child, and we can be so overpowered by this guilt that we are unable to function.

Anger and hostility are other dominant emotions that consume us like a raging fire. We're angry at what happened, at the perpetrator or perpetrators, and at all the things we are forced to deal with in order to apprehend and prosecute the killer. In our fragile, agitated state, we have to cope with the police, lawyers, and often the media. Our grief process is disrupted by the criminal justice procedures; our coping ability is strained by news coverage, the investigation, and a possible trial if a suspect is arrested. Whether our child was the intended victim or was just in the wrong place at the wrong time, murder or manslaughter takes a heavy psychological toll.

A variety of other situations might torment us: no arrest, rude treatment by police, no information from the police or the prosecutor, no notification of the trial date, not being allowed to attend part of the trial (we can be kept outside if we are a potential witness), a plea bargain for the killer with no explanation given to us, a defense attorney's slander of our child, the killer being free on bail while awaiting trial, a confession thrown out on a technicality, a lenient sentence, or a feeling that the police are no longer working on the case. These areas of aggravation make it impossible for us to make headway in our grieving.

In addition to the psychological burden we are carrying, we are plagued by financial concerns: funeral bills, psychiatric care for family members, medical care for our own health problems stemming from the trauma, the cost of private investigators and attorneys, the possible loss of pay if we are unable to function, the potential loss of scholarships for our remaining children if their grades fall because of how traumatized they are by their sibling's death, and even sometimes the logistics of moving to a new home to run away from the pain resulting from our family's rage or fear. Our whole world is compromised.

Parents of children killed by violence report that it often puts a heavy strain on a marriage. The suffering we are enduring might prevent us from being able to communicate effectively with our spouse or to draw support from him or her; blame hangs over each of our heads like a black cloud, ready to rain on us. When there is no sharing, no supporting, no comforting, we tend to become isolated and remote, shying away from our spouse and our family roles. Exhaustion takes over. We fall apart, depression sets in, and we have no interest in physical contact. We think we can bury the unrelenting pain by selling our home and divorcing our spouse, telling ourselves we are getting rid of all the memories. Hurt, blame, lack of communication, and a feeling of isolation can become a vicious cycle.

Although a high percentage of parents experience grave difficulties in their marriage while dealing with the killing of a child, some actually draw closer together, strengthening their bond and flatly refusing to let this intolerable act destroy any more of their life than it already has. With love and determination, they cling to each other with firm resolve to eliminate the obstacles to staying a team and continuing a meaningful life again. This is the ultimate tribute to their dead child: They refuse to become victims, as their child was.

After the death by violence of our child we parents need to seek help immediately. Many of us go to counselors, who can listen to our rage and frustration, which need to be expressed, but the most beneficial help will come from those people who have gone through the same kind of excruciating pain and the frustration of dealing with the criminal justice system. Finding a local chapter of Parents of Murdered Children or a similar support group gives us a chance to vent our frustrations, yell and scream, cuss and swear all we want in front of people who understand and who can be role models and helpful supporters on our journey. We get not only physical and emotional support but also knowledgeable assistance in understanding and dealing with police, lawyers, trials and the media. We also

> *The most beneficial help will come from those who have gone through the same kind of excruciating pain and the frustration of dealing with the criminal justice system.*

learn how to deal with the perpetrators—how to face them in court, be in the same room with them if we're giving a victim impact statement, deal with their lawyers and family, and organize efforts against their parole. We learn the process, the loopholes, the best ways to cope with anxiety and depression, and ways to manage the overwhelming feelings of revenge that dominate our thoughts day and night. We find supportive people who will share what has worked and not worked for them. They offer us hope—the hope to survive, and the hope of forgiving after the hate. We can find a sense of security, realizing that our feelings and emotions are genuine and indeed normal for what we have been through, and that all the counseling in the world will not rid us of these feelings. We are grateful to discover we are not alone at a time when we feel so scared, vulnerable, violated and distraught. We welcome fellow travelers into our life who can "walk the walk" with us.

Braving deaths from war and terrorism

The anguish of losing a child to war or terrorism mirrors much of the physical, mental and emotional pain that parents of murdered children face, especially regarding the violent and arbitrary nature of the death. But additional factors exacerbate this pain, such as constant local and national media coverage, endless public rituals and ceremonies, continual invasion of privacy at a time of vulnerability, and interminable paperwork to deal with insurance, death benefits and survivor funds.

Parents of children in the military usually are aware of the risks and dangers, especially during wartime. But no matter how mentally prepared we think we are, rarely are parents ready for the devastation we feel when the military officially informs us of the death of our child. Whether victim of enemy or friendly fire or a training accident, our child lies dead, usually far from home. It might take a lot of time and much red tape for the remains to be found and sent back to us; in some cases our child's body may never be found or released. These are some of the heartaches military parents face.

The big "Why?" is never answered, and haunts us like a repeating nightmare.

We are haunted by the imagery of our child's last moments in pain or fear and the fact that we were not able to be there to comfort them, to hold their hand, to embrace them in our arms, or to say a final goodbye. To know they were assaulted, mutilated or tormented in some way causes our feelings to explode like a bomb. We are in shock, denial and numbness; we experience agonizing physical and mental pain. We torture ourselves with questions: *Why did I encourage him or her to join the military? Why didn't I say no to him or her joining the reserves? Why didn't he or she have better training? Why are we in this war?* The big "Why?" is never answered, however, and haunts us like a repeating nightmare.

Compounding our grief could be battles with the military as we try to gather the facts to understand what caused the death of our child. It is especially hard for parents who experience a runaround or cover-up, even if it is done for valid security reasons. It is mind-boggling to find the military hostile or uncooperative as we try to piece together the details surrounding our child's death. If we have no body, it is easy for us to escape into denial, since it is hard for us to believe our child is really dead. Adding to our pain can be negative comments by fellow citizens who oppose the war or military action and seem to have no compassion for our loss or recognition of the fact that our child was protecting our country and everything we hold dear. Society's ignoring or minimizing of our loss is another bitter pill to swallow. We can be in emotional limbo waiting for paperwork to be completed, details to be confirmed, the body to be found and/or returned, and society to recognize our loss. This adds to the mountain of our grief.

If our child in the military was married, other factors can complicate the resolution of our grief. We parents are not considered the immediate next of kin; the spouse is. We are often left out of direct notification and other information. We are not involved in choosing the type and place of burial, planning the funeral ceremony, and sometimes, even having access to our grandchildren if our opinions differ from the spouse or we clash on any of the choices he or she has made.

In addition to formal military conflict, acts of terrorism have changed lives forever all around the globe. Whether it's U.S. ships, planes, military bases, embassies, government buildings or selected targets such as the World Trade Center in New York City, terrorist attacks are a wake-up call that what we term "normal" or "expected" can change in a heartbeat. The horrendous shock, the excruciating pain of loss, the raging anger, the loss of our innocence, and the fear of terror happening again all combine to assault our mind and body, overwhelming our ability to cope. These are normal reactions to an abnormal event, but they are magnified many times when the victims include our very own children.

September 11, 2001, is a date we will never forget. It was the first time so many noncombatants were killed simply because they reported to work. It was the first time since Pearl Harbor that the scope of loss completely shattered our confidence and we waited fearfully for the next shoe to drop. It was the first time the illusion of our invincibility literally collapsed in front of our eyes. The death and destruction were right there for all to see on TV—at the World Trade Center, the Pentagon, and site of the Flight 93 plane crash in Pennsylvania.

Many parents had no body to bury, no opportunity to establish the reality of the death, no sense of closure, no chance to say goodbye, no funeral, no grave to visit. One mother told me, "We are planning a funeral for my son, but I expect him to walk in the door any minute!" Because she didn't have his body, the wondering and the fantasizing about her child still being alive made her grieving an even much longer journey than it would have been if the body had been found.

One brokenhearted father whose son died in the World Trade Center and whose body was later found said in disbelief, "People tell me I'm *lucky*, because I got my son's body back." At a meeting of our chapter of The Compassionate Friends on Long Island, we all agreed that we never thought we would see the day when we would actually be grateful for having our child's body to bury. We never realized how much solace the body of our child provided us until September 11 showed us the alternative. (Some parents of murdered children and those of children in the military missing in action and presumed dead suffer this same fate of having no body to bury. They too never completely give up the hopeful fantasy that their child will someday return.)

Strong emotional reactions can interfere with our ability to function after suffering the death of our child due to terrorism. These stress reactions can appear immediately or come weeks or even months later. With understanding and support from loved ones, friends and colleagues, we parents try to deal with our fatigue, heartache, flashbacks, intrusive images, blame, nightmares, concentration problems, anxiety, depression, mood shifts, fear, panic, irritability, withdrawal, anger, guilt and emotional outbursts. Sometimes the traumatic event is so painful that we need assistance from a mental health professional. This in no way implies weakness or mental illness. It simply means this particular event of terror was too overwhelming for us to manage by ourselves.

Media coverage and public ceremonies and rituals in these cases can be both a blessing and a curse as we process our grief. To know our child has been remembered and "shared with the world" can be healing and comforting. However, some media concepts of grief contrast with our realities, adding to our upset and confusion. The media's frenetic race to bring "closure" belies the fact that there never really is closure. This loss is with us for life. It is a deep yearning that accompanies everything we do. Every day we work at adapting to life without our beloved child. One grieving father poignantly stated, "I won't have closure until they close the lid on *my* casket."

The media's continual pictures and reminders of the horrific event can repeatedly knock us down and even drive us into depression.

For some of us, the media's "hero halo" coverage of our child differs from the child we knew, causing a painful conflict in trying to deal with our true memories. The media's continual pictures and reminders of the horrific event can repeatedly knock us down and even drive us into depression. (I can't imagine what state I would be in if I had constantly seen newspaper photos of my children's car crashing into the open drawbridge. That image would have been imbedded in my mind forever without a moment's relief, certainly impeding my recovery. Critical-incident experts advise us to avoid reading newspaper accounts and watching repeated coverage of the traumatic event that caused our child's death.)

We must learn to pick and choose those rituals and cere-monies we feel will have meaning for us and give a boost to our hearts. We will learn to defeat the culture of death with emblems of life, with trees teeming with birds, with gardens and flowers, with acts of kindness, and with projects filled with the love we have for our child and are willing to share with oth-ers. We will find loving ways to soften the tremendous blow we have suffered after the tragic death of our child through the vio-lent acts of war or terrorism.

Even though I walk through the darkest valley,
I fear no evil; for you are with me;
your rod and your staff—
they comfort me.

Psalm 23:4

Cherishing the Seasons

I thank God every time I remember you.
Philippians 1:3

Celebrating birthdays and anniversaries

The calendar keeps turning and the world continues to do business as usual—even though our child has died. The birthdays and anniversaries appear sooner than we thought possible. These special days are hard for us, full of memories of all the things we used to do with our child and desire to bring that all back in an instant.

The first occurrences of these special days are always the hardest, because we are so aware of what we have lost and things we used to do with our child on that day. Birthdays and anniversaries are bittersweet—wonderful memories of our precious child combine with wanting him or her to be here right now. The longing lasts a lifetime, but for most of us its intensity diminishes as the years pass. We learn to celebrate the life of our child rather than dwell on his or her death, and that is a welcome joy to our heart.

Birthdays are especially difficult to face when our child is not there to be the center of attention. This once joyous day stirs up a myriad of memories attached to the pregnancy, birth and growing-up years of our child. Do we just forget about it, leave it off our calendars, and bury all the memories from past birthdays? Of course not. Even if we wanted to forget the day and the pain associated with it, our souls—and our true friends—won't let us.

Our child's birthday is still a special day in our life, one to be forever remembered. It's important to decide together as a family how to spend the day. Sometimes our plans involve compromise, since there could be different opinions. Some folks need quiet time, such as a long walk or hike, a jog along the beach, a visit to a church or a cemetery, or a drive in the country that gives them blessed time to reflect and remember. Others need the noise and companionship of friends, supportive hugs, and the comfort of favorite foods to survive the pain of the day. Some just have to keep busy—whether it's working, cooking, or visiting old haunts to relive happy memories. Others want to do new things and make new memories. We need to plan what is helpful to us, what we can handle, what might bring a little joy to our day.

Preparing the prayers, readings and music for these liturgies makes me feel that I am giving Peggy and Denis a beautiful birthday gift.

Ever since my children died, I have always had a morning Mass said on their birthdays at our church. For me it is a beautiful way to start the day. I always feel their overwhelming presence enveloping me, especially at the mention of the Communion of Saints and during Holy Communion. Sometimes I am the Lector or a Eucharistic Minister. That special involvement makes me feel even closer to my children, as if I am sharing a precious spiritual bond with them. Sometimes I invite friends and relatives to join us for the Mass and then for coffee or brunch at our house. On occasion my family has enjoyed a private Mass at home. Preparing the prayers, readings and music for these liturgies makes me feel that I am giving Peggy and Denis a beautiful birthday gift. It keeps my heart and mind busy and centered on my children on their special days, rather than on my sadness. Having something to look forward to on their birthdays seems to minimize my apprehension.

Each year our family plans a little different way of celebrating their birthdays. The festivities always include loving people, delicious food, a special prayer, a glowing candle, a birthday toast and a birthday cake. We also try to do something the "birthday child" enjoyed or something we like to do in memory of that child. It could be simply watching a favorite TV program or video, viewing home movies, eating at a restaurant he or she liked, attending a sporting event, shopping in old haunts, cooking a favorite meal, adding another rose bush to the garden, or doing an act of kindness in his or her memory. (Some parents in the early years of their grief take the day off from work just so they can relax and remember, cry all they want and savor the meaning of the day. Others make it a lifetime tradition for honoring their dead child.)

Sharing our child's birthday with others can be very comforting to us grieving parents. At our monthly meeting of The Compassionate Friends we have a special Birthday Table, where parents whose child's birthday is that month can put a picture or collage of the child or something symbolic of the child for us all to enjoy. Framed pictures, diplomas, trophies, awards, stuffed animals, quilts, wedding albums and such adorn the table, along with fresh flowers and lighted candles. Parents often bring gifts such as crocheted angels, fresh flowers, bookmarks, favorite candy, or copies of something their child wrote to give to those attending the meeting. A young mother whose infant daughter had died the year before brought each of us individual baby yellow tulips tied with yellow ribbons. Another mom and dad brought little bottles of champagne with their son's picture and birth and death dates printed on them. Near the end of the meeting, the "birthday parents" are invited to speak, telling everyone a little about their child. Many parents who never believed they could be public speakers are eager to get to the podium to "share their child with the world." One mother, new to the group, told me, "No way would I ever do that." But months later, when it was her son's birthday, she couldn't wait to tell the group about her child. To add to the celebration, many of the parents also bring a birthday cake, their child's favorite cookies, wine or some special food for our refreshment table. The Birthday Table has become a very important part of our meeting, validating our children's existence and allowing us to celebrate their special day with people who understand. The round of applause after each speech always brings smiles all around the room.

Some birthdays seem harder than others. For some reason, milestones—such as ten, thirteen, "sweet sixteen," twenty-one, twenty-five, thirty—are more painful than others. They are major celebrations with our child that we have been denied, and our whole being feels it, especially when we see our friends observing these particular birthdays with their children. It's especially important to plan ahead for these milestone days to make sure we don't find ourselves all alone, down in the dumps, falling apart, or curled up in the fetal position.

Receiving thoughtful cards from dear relatives and friends who are remembering our child's birthday deeply touches us each year, especially after the first few years have passed and most major support has dwindled. A simple card or written message, even an e-mail, can add a glow to our day, reminding us that someone remembers our child and cares about us.

Anniversaries of the death of our child always recall the events leading up to it, no matter how many years have passed. Most outsiders don't understand that, thinking that only the first few years are painful. But we parents never forget the circumstances surrounding our child's death, and we relive them at each anniversary, not because we want to be maudlin but because it's human nature. We couldn't avoid it, even if we tried. So, just like with birthdays, it helps to plan ahead so that we will be doing something that helps our heart get through the day. The odd thing is that we are usually so uptight about the approaching anniversary that we usually find the days preceding it harder for us than the anniversary itself. The pain of the day that we were so afraid of doesn't seem to materialize, and somehow we get through the anniversary in one piece. Still, we must remember to be gentle and patient with ourselves on those days. We learn that time itself does not heal; it's what we do with the time. That's why some planning is so important.

As with birthdays, we need to discuss options for the day with our family. Will it include a special religious service, a gathering of friends, a special meal, a visit to the cemetery, a planting in the garden, a release of balloons, a dedication of a monument, an announcement of a special project initiated in memory of our child? Whatever we plan—whether it's something major, such as establishing a scholarship or starting a foundation, or something as simple as having lunch with friends—marking the anniversary day with a special event will keep our child remembered.

Tears can fall and that's OK, because tears bring a sense of release and healing. The funny thing is that the tears are a mixture of happiness and sadness that we can't separate. They are a combination of tears of joy for the memories we have that fill our hearts and tears of sorrow because we wish our child were still here with us. Anniversaries and birthdays are a time to share with others the special love we have for our child. Doing that keeps their memories alive and makes us feel so much better.

Coping with the holidays

The hearts of bereaved parents fill with apprehension as holidays approach. How careful we have to be not to waste our precious energy running away from them. Instead we must learn to lean into the pain. It cannot be outrun. We need to let the grief process run *Holidays are not* its full course—there are no shortcuts. *a time to put on*

We parents used to celebrate various *a mask of phony* holidays with our child, and now we have to reweave that big hole we feel in *smiles.* our family fabric. During the holidays we need to express our emotions and tell others what we need in order to function. Holidays are not a time to put on a mask of phony smiles.

The Pilgrims' first Thanksgiving wasn't just a three-day feast. It was a powerful ritual that not only mourned horrific losses (more than half of their party died in the first year) but also recognized the possibility of recovery after loss. Their shared meal celebrated the ability of human beings to triumph over death through the strength of community. The survivors came together in loving support and faith to move forward toward life and growth. We can do the same at Thanksgiving and other festive times—gather together as we struggle through pain to give thanks for love and lives shared. We can sustain hope by embracing new people and new strategies.

We must begin to know our own strength, even while realizing we can't do all the things we did before, at least not yet. We just don't have the energy. Making some little changes in holiday traditions can help us. We might simplify the meal by shortening the guest list, by having everybody bring a dish, by serving three courses instead of six, by using paper plates instead of the good china, or by planning a buffet rather than a formal sit-down dinner. We might want to have the meal catered, or go to someone else's home, or try a restaurant. We might entrust the entire holiday plans to another family member and just enjoy being a guest, without any pressure or panic attacks over shopping, cleaning, cooking or serving.

With every decision we make, we begin to take back control of our life.

We have to choose what appeals to us that makes each holiday doable. Taking charge in little ways helps bring back our confidence and self-esteem. With every decision we make, we begin to take back control of our life.

We can evaluate our family traditions, choosing the ones that give us a lift and leaving out the ones that make us feel like a steamroller just ran over us. For example, we might put up our nativity scene and forget about the Christmas tree. We might invite others to put up our tree or help decorate it. We might choose to have a three-foot tree instead of our traditional eight-footer. We might decide to skip making Christmas cookies or bake just a few kinds. We can choose not to buy presents and stay out of malls and department stores altogether, or we might order through catalogs or online. We might want to make something special in memory of our child to give to others. We might break the tradition of attending midnight Mass, realizing our energy level is too low to make it that late or just because we want to start a new tradition. We can skip Christmas cards or find solace in sending ones with just the right wording. We have to make choices that help our heart get through these festive occasions.

I have found great comfort in angels since Peggy and Denis died. Our Christmas tree is covered with them, and I always find a precious angel card to send to my closest friends. In those first years after my children's deaths, I did not have the heart or energy to go Christmas shopping, but some little angels in one store caught my eye and I fell in love with them. They made me smile. I bought batches of them—six of this kind, ten of that. I had hundreds of angels on my kitchen table. Joe never complained or told me to quit buying them; he was thrilled that I had found a mission. With passion I inscribed my children's names and anniversary dates on each angel and then gifted them to all our friends and relatives. I was consumed with fiery energy to have everyone I knew remember my children that Christmas by putting one of these angels on their tree or mantel. I imagined that when they took the angel out of its box, they would remember Peggy and Denis and perhaps say a little prayer for them. I've continued this loving tradition every year, always including the current year and the words "Remembering Peggy and Denis." I'm afraid my angels are taking over my best friends' trees now, since they've received a new one every year since 1986, but they don't seem to mind my little ritual—in fact, they look forward each year to seeing what the new angel will be.

That first Christmas, just four months after Peggy and Denis died, Annie asked if we were going to put up the tree. "How do you feel about it?" I asked her. She said, "I think it will be hard, but it would be harder not to." Joe and I felt the same way. Peggy and Denis loved Christmas, so we all agreed that very first Christmas to decorate the house with all the trimmings in their memory. We have done so every year since then, bringing us all joy, along with some healthy tears. We also hold an open house every year during the Christmas holidays for our Compassionate Friends. Some of the parents in the group cannot face putting up a Christmas tree or even think of decorating, but they're able to come and thoroughly enjoy the warmth and comforting atmosphere of our home.

At one Compassionate Friends meeting a mother asked the group if her family should hang their dead son's Christmas stocking. She was vacillating between hanging it up and retiring it, until she learned a beautiful custom from another bereaved parent. That mother said, "We hang up our son's stocking and fill it with love notes and good deeds done in his memory. It's a great place to empty our hearts at Christmas-time." I heard that suggestion and wondered why I hadn't thought of that. I went home and unpacked Peggy's and Denis' stockings; it felt good to include them again in the row hanging over the fireplace in our living room. Just seeing their names there made me smile.

Including our deceased children in holiday festivities keeps them very much with us. We can make them part of the holiday by telling favorite stories about them at the dinner table, lighting a special candle in their honor at the beginning of the festive meal or before the first present is opened, leaving out an album of favorite pictures for all to enjoy and chat about, sharing music they loved, making a centerpiece filled with treasured items of theirs, reading a poem or sharing an anecdote that zeroes in on their personality, or donating to someone in need in their memory. It helps some parents' hearts to buy a present they know their child would have loved and contribute it to a gift drive, hoping to bring joy to a child of the same age as their deceased son or daughter.

Bad days can get us down, and holidays can exacerbate our feelings of sadness. This goes with the territory, and the territory is named "grief." We can't walk *around* grief; we have to walk *through* it. So we can't let anything minor ruin our day. What could be worse than what we have already suffered? We try to think positively; we choose life. We surround ourselves with people who offer us vitality. We stay at arm's length from those who pull down our spirits with demands or insensitive advice. We choose things that give us satisfaction, even if they seem crazy to others. If we want to hang lights on a tree in our front yard in memory of our child and leave them on all year round, that's all right. Anything that gives our heart a lift is good for us to do. That might include decorating our child's grave for the different holidays. Whether it's a plastic turkey, a singing wreath, a miniature Christmas tree, or a fluffy Easter bunny, our hearts will feel a lot better when we share the holiday with our child.

During holiday seasons we need to set goals for ourselves

that are easy to attain, and we need to congratulate ourselves every time we achieve one of them and forgive ourselves when we don't. We're beginners. Success takes time. We learn as we go along the journey. For example, instead of a four-hour holiday visit with your relatives, try two hours. Be flexible and feel the strength of achieving a simple goal you have set for yourself. It's a big morale booster.

Doing something for others in our child's name is a magnificent way to add a glow to our holidays. Do what you feel comfortable doing and what brings meaning to you. You can cook meals, volunteer at food pantries, check on shut-ins, or assist in hospitals. You can drive, shovel, telephone, mow, clean, trim, deliver, type, greet and perform countless other tasks for others, depending on your interests and abilities. One bereaved dad volunteered his Christmas Eve to sit beside the bed of a hospitalized child so the parents could spend the evening at home with their other children. Remembering our child through acts of kindness brings real meaning to our loss. Holidays will always be rough, but we can find ways to sprinkle love—and even a little joy—into them.

Remembering our child through acts of kindness brings real meaning to our loss.

Remembering on "Hallmark days"

All families have favorite days to celebrate. We all know the ones that mean the most to us. Before they died, many of our children brought home artwork and projects to touch our hearts on Valentine's Day, Mother's Day, Father's Day, Halloween and all the other celebrations children love. We bereaved parents shouldn't forget all those occasions. We will feel the absence of our child as these "Hallmark days" pop up on the calendar. We might have younger children or grandchildren who are still fascinated with these occasions or older children who want to carry on the longtime traditions. What do we do now? Can we enjoy these special days or do we simply ignore them?

Before Peggy and Denis died, our family could find hundreds of reasons to celebrate. You could find us walking around sporting party hats on the dog's birthday or gobbling up ice cream sundaes to celebrate a Notre Dame touchdown. The class I taught at school was known as "the party class"—quick to celebrate tests passed, books read, perfect attendance and other happy events. So observing "Hallmark days" was second nature to our family. Early on, Joe, Annie and I decided to continue observing them. We were still alive, and we knew Peggy and Denis would be downright disappointed in us if we were to stop living as such. I even got a chuckle remembering the time Peggy called me from college after I sent her a cute little Easter basket overflowing with goodies. She begged me to send two more for her roommates, whose families didn't bother with "that stuff" anymore. So we continued to send valentines, bake Irish soda bread, color Easter eggs, carve pumpkins and do all the fun things that had brought us warm fuzzy feelings before Peggy and Denis died. As we honored the traditions we had established, we were able to remember the joy we had shared on those occasions. With some searching we were even able to find some of the cards, gifts and photos from past celebrations to place in our Memory Box. We don't want to forget the happy times or the love from all those festive events. We still want to have a meaningful life filled with love and laughter.

We don't want to forget the happy times or the love from all those festive events.

Some grieving families find it hard to celebrate anything. They need time to sort out their feelings and to decide the path they will follow on their journey. There is no rush. We go at our own pace. We are all different, but we follow the same rule of thumb: Do what helps your heart. Some families will establish new traditions on these days that will allow them to breathe easier and help fill an empty spot in their lives. Others might need the help of a counselor to explore why they are "stuck" in their grief. We must learn to cry when we have to and to laugh when we can. Sometimes that is the gift of "Hallmark days."

Sharing others' joy

When our heart feels broken and we have to use all our strength just to get out of bed in the morning, we are overwhelmed when we receive an invitation to a joyful event. We wrestle with ourselves. We ask ourselves: *Will we be able to fit in? Can we make it through the event without breaking down? Will we cry and embarrass ourselves? Will we feel like a fish out of water? Can we really "celebrate"? Are they expecting too much from us? Are we dishonoring our child by taking part? Can we really get dressed up and smile? Do we want people pointing at us and whispering our story to one another? How long do we have to stay? Can we handle being surrounded by happy people?* Only we can answer how we feel and what our gut reaction is to sharing others' joy.

Some of us feel a commitment to the people who were there for us in our hours of sorrow, and we want very much to be there for them in their time of joy. We want to show them how much we appreciate their support by lending our presence to their event, even if it's just for a short time. We feel as if we would walk through fire for them, and we want them to know that. We find comfort in whatever gives our world meaning, and if that means celebrating with a friend, we do it.

Some invitations, however, come from people who have not been there for us, who have not contributed to our healing. We might not want to go out of our way to join them for their special occasion, and that's all right. Sometimes we have to listen to what our heart can handle. If we are not ready to socialize with certain people, we need to decline the invitation without heaping guilt on ourselves. For such events we simply reply with a guilt-free "no."

Other occasions are just too painful for us to participate in. With loving hearts we have to convey our regrets "until we feel stronger." This could include an invitation to a christening for those of us who have lost a baby, a First Communion for those who have lost a young child, a graduation for those who have lost a high school or college student, or an engagement party or wedding for those of us who have lost a young adult. It may be just too difficult to share the joy that we want so desperately to be ours. We may feel so cheated and our pain may be so raw that we know we are not yet ready to be part of the celebration. We have to set realistic goals, and it is realistic to know that we need more time to face some situations.

In 1995, nine years after Peggy and Denis died, I attended with no second thought the 30th birthday party of a dear friend's son. Enjoying a delightful party filled with loving friends, I stood to sing "Happy Birthday" at cake-cutting time and was blindsided with uncontrollable tears streaming down my face. I suddenly realized that this would also have been the year of my son's 30th birthday. I was caught off-guard. Grief can ambush us even after many years and at times when we think we are completely in control.

Even though I was determined to attend them, for years I found weddings to be hard as I watched cousins' and friends' children walk down the aisle. I cried like a baby in the church and then was fine at the reception. I just needed that one time for release of all my frustration and anguish. I learned to carry big handkerchiefs! Some grieving parents, on the other hand, do fine at the wedding ceremony but crumble at the reception when the father of the bride dances with his daughter or the mother of the groom dances with her son. Attending ceremonies that might have included our child—such as confirmations, graduations or weddings—usually brings heart-rending tears. Watching our remaining children marry, with a brother or sister missing from the wedding party, also creates a bittersweet occasion for us.

It is important for us not to be ashamed of our grief on these joyful occasions. We are merely mourning the child we loved. Our whole heart and soul wants him or her to be physically present for the celebration. There is no need to apologize for grieving. We are doing the best we can, working toward a healthy understanding that our child survives as part of us.

All major loss is dealt with in tiny steps. No one absorbs it all at once. It takes time to work our way through the pain, fear, sadness and rage that accompany the loss of our child. Support comes from special places that talk to our soul, from healing activities that buoy us. We have to learn to do what feels right and good for us. Even those of us who have lost a child can appreciate the moment and claim a small portion of life's joy.

Planning get-away vacations

Anything we do to get away from the pain can be considered a "vacation" from our grief, although we don't have to actually travel to enjoy the benefits. The secret is to find the things that bring a respite from our intense grieving.

After the deaths of my two children, I found that staying with the familiar made me feel comfortable. Having my support circle nearby was important to me. Enjoying the things I had shared with Peggy and Denis kept them close to my heart. Even though tears could accompany these pleasures, the tears were healing. Whether it was simply walking along the beach where we had had so many family outings, sitting by the pool where we had spent so many hours with the swim team, watching a soccer game (which took so much of our time with three athletes in the family), eating at favorite restaurants, or cheering for

Some families agonize over whether to go away for a vacation after the death of their child; others can't get away fast enough.

favorite teams (the New York Mets, New York Islanders and Notre Dame), these things lifted my spirits and reinforced my children's presence in my heart. So even though I was at home, I enjoyed the refreshing benefits of a real vacation.

Some families agonize over whether to go away for a vacation after the death of their child; others can't get away fast enough. How differently we grieve! Sometimes a compromise is necessary for spouses and family members with different needs.

Some families book travel reservations for every major holiday; others plan only an annual vacation. If taking a cruise, flying to a distant sunny haven, or just relaxing at a nearby resort helps you gain a moment of peace, do it. But don't go alone. There is a need to reflect or quietly meditate wherever you are, but when you are hurting so terribly it is not wise to be alone for long periods of time. It is good to have someone with whom to share your thoughts and release some of those feelings that are haunting you. Having a good listener with you on vacation is the best medicine. It also provides someone to hug. Author and speaker Doug Manning's prescription is four hugs a day for survival, eight hugs for maintenance, twelve hugs for growth. So make sure you vacation with the right person!

Sometimes a change of venue is just what we need.

Many of us find solace in a trip away from our home base. Sometimes a change of venue is just what we need. A little sunshine can warm our souls, so maybe the warmer climates will appeal to us. Sun lovers seem to accomplish ten times as much on a bright day, so a sunny vacation might be very rewarding for us. Maybe the invitation of sailing, swimming or just plain relaxing on a chaise lounge might tempt us. Others might relish the invigorating climate of a snowy region and look forward to the physical demands of skiing, snowboarding or ice-skating. Some might prefer the great outdoors and the rigors of camping, while others choose the variety of distractions a big city offers. All of us are looking for a timeout from our grief, a diversion from our pain, a few hours of reviving our spirit, and empowerment to go on with life.

Some of us find solace in visiting places that were dear to our child or where our whole family spent many happy moments. We might go back to the familiar beach resort, amusement park, ski lodge, dude ranch, timeshare condo, baseball stadium, museum, theater or golf course to capture those warm feelings from the past. Reliving those precious times seems to make the memories somehow indelible, never to be forgotten. Those memories help create a permanent link to the past, which nurtures our grieving hearts. Others of us find it too painful to visit vacation spots that once were a great source of happiness. We miss our child too much in those familiar settings, so we prefer to explore new places and begin new experiences from which to draw our strength for the "new normal" we are creating. That is perfectly fine; each of us does what helps us most.

In the early days of my grief it was very painful for me to leave home—my "nest," as I called it—whether it was for a few minutes or a few hours. To avoid becoming a hermit, I found great comfort in preparing a pocket photo album filled with my favorite pictures of my children, just like a grandma's "brag book." By carrying it with me in every pocketbook I used, wherever I went, I felt I had Peggy and Denis with me. I didn't have to look at it, but I could if I wanted to, and I could show it to anyone if I wished to talk about my children. It broke the ice, soothed my heart, and kept my children close to me. For some reason this album became my security blanket in those dark days and gave me the strength to leave the house with them "in tow." As time went on, I found that I no longer needed to take the album with me—Peggy and Denis were now with me in my heart. Today the album lays on the night table next to my bed, a healthy reminder of how I have grown in my grief. Others have tried this suggestion, cramming a little album full of their child's favorite pictures as they left on a vacation they didn't really want to take. They returned happily announcing that it indeed had made a difference, allowing them to release some of the emptiness they had felt and to feel the presence of their child in the place they were visiting.

Go your way, eat the fat and drink sweet wine...
for this day is holy to our Lord;
and do not be grieved,
for the joy of the Lord is your strength.

Nehemiah 8:10

Rescuing Forgotten Mourners

Comfort, O comfort my people, says your God.
Isaiah 40:1

Acknowledging loss from miscarriage or stillbirth

What do we parents do when miscarriage or stillbirth suddenly rips the hopes and dreams we had for our long-awaited baby from us? How do we face the fact that our precious miracle of life is gone before he or she had a chance to flourish? What was supposed to be a time of celebration, a time of welcoming, a time of happiness, has become one of tears, sadness and isolation. Our grief needs to be validated by others, not ignored or minimized with the thought, often incorrect, that we can always get pregnant again.

For all of us—especially those who were eagerly looking forward to the arrival of their firstborn and those who had experienced difficulty conceiving—such a loss turns our world upside down, leaving us feeling shattered and vulnerable. The good news is that over the years society has come to understand how real such a loss is for parents. Years ago nothing was said; no rituals were performed. You just went on with life and pretended it never happened. Families did not talk about the loss; it was swept under the rug and you kept your grief to yourself. Spouses did not share their sense of devastation with each other. Babies were not named, support groups did not exist, and few books were available to help parents understand what they were experiencing. You wonder how earlier generations got the strength to go on after enduring so much loss.

As a young bride, I suffered the loss of three babies in mid-pregnancy from 1969 to 1972. My saving grace was that I already had three young children I could hug and for whom I could thank God. I hoped we would be blessed with more—a wish that was not in the Lord's plan. I rationalized the situation shortly after my third miscarriage, when my former husband was stricken with a serious heart condition and I became the breadwinner with three children under five years of age. "God knew," I told myself. But if I hadn't had my other children, I know that rationalization would never have comforted me.

I probably am finally grieving for the three babies I lost long ago, the ones society and circumstances never allowed me to mourn openly.

Today I am a facilitator for the Guardian Angel Perinatal Support Group, which is a local chapter of SHARE, a diocesan support organization for parents who have lost a child to miscarriage, stillbirth or infant death. I console many parents who have lost a baby. I have learned so much from these courageous young mothers and fathers, who give each other support and hope, and I probably am finally grieving for the three babies I lost long ago, the ones society and circumstances never allowed me to mourn openly.

There is much more help available today for perinatal loss, especially through national support groups such as Empty Cradle, SHARE and The Compassionate Friends. In addition, hospitals, hospice groups, local agencies and congregations offer help and support, and the Internet offers a wealth of chat rooms, Web sites and online support.

Parents are no longer isolated from each other; they can talk about their loss, question their doctors and access medical information more easily. They also can share their anger, guilt and frustrations. They name their babies, have rituals for them, and talk openly about their children. All these actions affirm their loss and help keep their child permanently counted as a family member.

Hospitals now allow and encourage parents to see, touch, and even hold their child after a miscarriage or stillbirth. They can sit and rock the child and tell him or her what is in their hearts. There is no rush. The hospitals want the parents to remember these special moments, to make this child real to them. Some hospitals now issue a "certificate of life," a ritual acknowledgement rather than a legal one, recognizing that the parents indeed suffered the loss of a baby. Eight states now issue a "Certificate of Birth Resulting in Stillbirth," prompted by passage of the "MISSing Angels Bill" to acknowledge the existence of these babies. (MISS stands for Mothers in Sympathy and Support.)

Some parents fill a Memory Box, a small box used to hold precious items such as footprints, pictures, videotapes, blankets, tiny T-shirts, locks of hair, name ID bracelets, and sonograms. Special items like this signify that the baby existed. Naming the baby can help confirm that reality. It is never too late. I did it 30 years later, using the names I had chosen long before—Matthew, Patrick and Maria.

A memorial ceremony can affirm a miscarriage or stillbirth so that relatives and friends can recognize the loss and offer their loving support. Today, through hard-earned legislation, families can request the remains of an unborn child for private burial, something that was never even considered years ago.

Planting a tree or garden, unveiling a plaque or funding a special cause in the baby's name can keep a child from being erased from people's minds. October 15 is Pregnancy and Infant Loss Remembrance Day. To promote this occasion, more and more hospitals are offering annual programs to recognize and mourn babies lost to miscarriage, stillbirth or infant death. At these ceremonies, parents might be asked to write thoughts about their lost children or to hang a name or a memory on a specially designated wall to add their children's presence to the gathering. Their children's names might be inscribed on special bricks in a hospital memorial garden. Parents might participate in a balloon release. These rituals acknowledge the loss and help them face the reality of their child's death.

The movement to commemorate pregnancy losses is driven in large part by the growing numbers of older women who, having put off childbearing, find themselves facing great difficulty trying to conceive and carry a baby to term. When they become pregnant, often with the help of fertility drugs and treatments, their joy at having bucked the odds is boundless. But if their pregnancies fail, they are devastated by the loss of the child and by the fear that the chance to bear another is fading.

At a funeral or a wake for the death of a child who has survived birth for even a few weeks, there's usually a wealth of support for the parents. But when a child dies in the hospital and never comes home, no one knows what to do. Nobody wants to add to the parents' sorrow, so they offer their condolences and then stop talking about the loss. I can still feel the emptiness of my arms leaving the hospital three times after my miscarriages with no baby to cuddle. I remember thinking, "They didn't even give me a teddy bear to hug!"

The Roman Catholic Church has a rite, the Mass of Angels, to mourn children who have not reached the age of reason. That would include any unborn child, of course, since the Church holds that life begins at conception. But the Mass is rarely offered, due to cultural discomfort and because most parents are not even aware of such an opportunity to grieve the loss of their child.

It is up to the bereaved parents to decide what type of ritual will best help their hearts. One family planted an evergreen on the due date of the baby they lost and gets comfort watching it grow and mature, always reminding them of their precious son who died after being born prematurely. To remember their child who died in the womb, another couple lit a candle each evening—"a way to light the darkness," they said. They felt the candle was lighting their way forward. The simple ritual became a symbol of healing and hope for them and an inspiration that they would move on and have a baby one day. It had a positive, motivating message for their broken hearts.

One mother whose husband and parents tried to rush her through her grief after a miscarriage at six months needed a way to deal with her unexpressed pain. She had engraved a gold identification bracelet with the name—Maria—that she had planned to give to her daughter when she grew up, and the woman now wears it herself every day. Often, as she had hoped, it prompts people to ask her who Maria is, giving her a chance to talk about her lost daughter.

Some parents plant gardens to remember the precious baby they lost, receiving comfort from the blossoms that bring new life each year and affirm the opportunity for new growth. Others wear a locket with a picture or a strand of their baby's hair tucked inside—something to help them make sure they never forget their child. Some parents who have delivered a stillborn child find an artist to paint a portrait from the single hospital baby picture they have. They proudly hang the picture in a prominent place in their home, sharing the child no one had the opportunity to know. Others who have suffered a miscarriage have a print of their baby's sonogram beautifully framed, announcing to the world that this baby will always be remembered as part of their family. The goal is not to depress others or solicit their pity, but simply to tell the world how important it is to them that their baby be remembered.

Blood problems, genetic diseases and other specific issues can be addressed with information gathered after the loss of a child.

Loss of a child to miscarriage or stillbirth triggers the all-consuming question "Why?" which never gets answered the way parents want it to be. But parents do seek to understand the causes of what happened. Many times medical reasons can be found that can insure a better chance at delivering a healthy baby in the future. Blood problems, genetic diseases and other specific issues can be addressed with information gathered after the loss of a child. Some parents might be directed to doctors who specialize in high-risk pregnancies. Many times a baby's death allows parents to uncover medical conditions about themselves or their other children that they didn't know. This knowledge often lifts some of the burden from their hearts by recognizing that the baby made a real contribution to the family, even in his or her death.

Parents who suffer the unexpected death of their baby from Sudden Infant Death Syndrome (SIDS) feel particularly frustrated and angry because no one really knows why SIDS occurs; there are no medical answers, no specific symptoms or cure, no preventive measures, no warning. Parents tuck a healthy child into bed, only to find a cold, still child in the crib the next time they check. Adding to the pain of unexpected infant death is the length of time it can take to get an autopsy report. Many times after the long wait parents are told that the findings are inconclusive. No amount of information can change the outcome, of course, but parents need all the information and the clearest explanation as promptly as physicians and hospital staff can provide it. Without such facts parents tend to blame themselves needlessly.

Spouses grieve differently, which can create severe communication problems.

Just like parents who have lost older children, couples dealing with the loss of their baby might experience changes in their marital relationship, energy level, social life, and sexual desire, and loss of interest in their usual daily activities. They can be in shock, denial, protest, depression, confusion or combinations of these. Spouses grieve differently, which can create severe communication problems. Women are used to talking about their heartache; men seem to pride themselves on keeping everything hidden inside. Mothers cry and fathers rage, and many fathers keep busy with work or friends to avoid the tears at home. Women enjoyed the relationship with the growing baby within them, men considered themselves the protector of the baby—and both feel guilty for the loss of the child.

Only heartfelt communication can overcome such self-blame. After miscarriage or the delivery of a stillborn child, mothers usually suffer the mood swings of hormones gone awry; fathers might not understand the random tearful outbursts these can cause. Journaling is helpful for these couples if they can write about all their feelings and unload all their frustrations. When it's hard to talk to their spouse they can simply show them their journal and allow the great power of written words to break the ice. One mother who suffered four miscarriages said, "My journaling took the form of letters to my husband expressing my grief. I think they helped our marriage survive this very difficult time. Writing became an avenue of much needed communication, a safe haven for those thoughts and feelings that could otherwise become overwhelming. My letters were there for him to read and re-read, and later when I felt stronger they were there for us to discuss."

Any miscarriage, stillbirth or infant death, whether sudden or anticipated, through illness or accident, is a devastating experience for parents. We feel intense pain when we look at the empty crib, the vacant bedroom, the lonesome toys, the unworn clothing, the vanished dreams. Having others recognize this heartbreaking loss, offer their support, and allow us to grieve at our own pace in our own way helps our healing process greatly.

Honoring the love of an estranged or divorced parent

My former husband and I had been divorced for four years when Peggy and Denis died. We were fortunate that we were able to make decisions together after their deaths without any upsetting disagreements. Together we made the funeral arrangements, chose the readings and music for the Masses, and handled the myriad details that had to be addressed.

All divorced couples that lose a child, however, do not share our experience. Major decisions have to be made that should involve both parents, but many times these decisions become a tug of war that adds to the unbearable pain both parents are feeling. Clashes can result over which religion to observe, which funeral home to use, whether to bury or cremate the body, and what kind of service to have. There can be disagreement over the celebrant, readings, music, who will deliver the eulogy, who will perform special roles at the funeral, and the final resting place for the child. If family cemetery plots are involved, parents must somehow reach agreement on which one to use. If a new plot is to be selected, parents ought to agree where it will be and who will hold the deed. If a meal is to be served after the funeral, where will it be and who will attend? Later on, choosing a headstone or marker with a specific inscription will involve parental input and perhaps more compromise. Footing the many funeral bills (and other expenses, such as doctor or hospital bills) is another source of possible conflict that adds to estranged parents' pain.

When the parents live in separate households, sometimes with a new family involved, people seem to rush to support the parent with whom the child lived, usually the mother, and hesitate to offer the same help to the other parent, usually the father. Both parents have lost a precious child, but in many cases lines of division seem to be drawn, never to be crossed. It seems a shame that in time of sorrow, relatives and friends can't bury the hatchet and respond to the terrible loss suffered by both parents. All bereaved parents need their loss to be acknowledged; all need a loving support system; no one needs the extra pain of not having his or her grief recognized. Parents who are divorced or separated might no longer love each other, but that does not mean they no longer love their children. In many cases they have become bonded even more strongly with their children in order to fill the void of the missing spouse.

Many times, fruit baskets, casseroles, food platters or flowers are delivered to the home where the child lived and nothing is sent to the other parent. Even if both parents come together to be with relatives and friends at the child's home, it is an empty feeling for the non-custodial parent to return home and find nothing from relatives and friends that separately acknowledges his or her grief. Sometimes people just don't realize that two households have to be acknowledged, that two parents are hurting, and that both of them need individual attention.

There are also situations in which for a variety of reasons a parent has had little or no contact with the child since leaving the family. It is very hard for that parent to return for the funeral, and family members rarely greet him or her with open arms. No matter what age the child was when he or she died, the estranged biological parent has regrets for things not done and opportunities missed, for dreams and hopes gone up in smoke. This is not a time for cruelty, revenge, getting even, or taking sides. This is a time to realize that a child of two parents has died and that both need comforting.

Bereaved parents who are divorced or separated might in fact have a good working relationship and be able to give each other mutual support and make the arrangements for their child's funeral with a minimum of conflict. But after the funeral, if no new spouse or partner is involved, each must deal with the death of his or her child as a single parent. All single parents miss the special physical and emotional support, the tender touch, and simply the compassionate listening that only a loving spouse can provide. The death of a child is not an easy road for single parents, but joining a support group can help them find others who understand their pain, will listen to their story, share what works for them, and offer hope and friendship. They do not have to walk the journey of grief alone; in a support group their grief will be acknowledged and understood.

Confirming that siblings hurt too

Family and friends seem to rally around us bereaved parents, but often they offer little support to our other children—the brothers and sisters who have lost a sibling. That's why siblings have been called "the forgotten mourners." Over and over again, our remaining children are asked to "take care of mom and dad" and "be strong," but so many people fail to recognize their loss. Losing a brother or sister affects a person forever.

Losing a brother or sister affects a person forever.

Siblings, both young and old, have definite needs in their grief. They have new responsibilities and a new place in the family hierarchy. For example, if the oldest or youngest child has died, another child now assumes that position. In many cases the remaining sibling becomes an only child. All at the same time, our remaining daughter Annie became the oldest, remained the youngest, and was the only living child in our family. She had been the baby of the family for 18 years, delighting in the laughter, companionship and shenanigans of an older brother and sister. She was suddenly all alone. Three weeks after we buried Peggy and Denis, Annie left to start her freshman year at a college 200 miles away, knowing nobody and having no built-in support system there. I depended on the telephone and made sure there was a letter or card in her mailbox every day. (How I wish we had had e-mail at that time!) I knew she was in pain, and I did everything I could to "walk the walk" with her from a distance.

As we parents struggle to cope with the death of our child, our remaining children are doing the same thing. They need our love and support to get through the loss of their sibling, even while we are grieving ourselves. It's important to be open and honest with our remaining children about the cause and nature of their brother's or sister's death (even if it was a suicide) in an age-appropriate way. Kids need facts as much as we need them, so we must state things as simply as possible—not glossing over details or speaking in riddles. We must welcome their questions and be honest when we don't have the answers. We have to let them voice their feelings of guilt, anger, loneliness and sadness by becoming loving listeners for them.

Kids need facts as much as we need them, so we must state things as simply as possible.

The main thing we bereaved parents can do for our remaining children is to give them permission to grieve. We can model our grief for them by letting them observe us talking openly about the death, reaching out to others for comfort, and praying. They need to know that crying is perfectly natural, that they never need to apologize for feeling sad. Don't ask them to have a stiff upper lip. Give them the luxury of telling the world how they really feel. Remind them they don't have to wear a "happy mask."

Children old enough to love are old enough to grieve. Depending on their age, we should include siblings in funeral preparations, perhaps helping us choose burial clothing, floral pieces, favorite items to be tucked into the casket, and photographs to be displayed. We should invite their input for the funeral service regarding possible pallbearers, music, prayers, readings and people to include. (Annie was involved in all those decisions.)

On the other hand, we need to honor the siblings' request if they can't or don't want to be part of making these decisions. They, too, need to grieve in their own way and on their own timetable. Remember, they may have become truly aware of mortality for the first time in their lives. They may be thinking "Who's next" or maybe even "I'm next," which can be a paralyzing feeling for children.

Very young children may not want to attend the wake or the funeral, and they probably should not be forced to do so. But they should be encouraged. Although it might be difficult for them to see their sibling in an open casket, it can be physical proof to them that their brother or sister died. Being surrounded with loving family and friends at the wake can offer them time to talk, to feel the reality of the death, and to hear all the stories people share about their sister or brother, allowing them to store up a mountain of memories. Being a part of the rituals makes the death more real for them at a time when they might be tempted to be in denial.

When we return home after the burial, it is important that we provide an atmosphere that will allow siblings to express their feelings and thoughts over an extended period of time. We should allow opportunities for them to grieve together with us, to grieve alone, and to grieve with their own friends. We must also let them share unfinished business, such as the burden of unhappy exchanges, harsh words, or disagreements with their brother or sister. We must allow them to get guilty feelings out in the open and talk about unpleasant memories. Most of all we must avoid putting their deceased sibling on an unrealistic pedestal to the point that he or she becomes unrecognizable.

We also must resist the impulse to clip our remaining children's wings under the guise of protecting them. (Despite outsiders' advice to the contrary, we gave Annie the choice to follow her dreams, rather than putting a butterfly net over her to keep her safe and by our side. Annie thrived on the loose rein we allowed her.) Siblings are entitled to their life choices and the freedom to pursue their own interests. They need room to develop their new identity, to make choices, and to reach for the stars.

As parents we can help our remaining children most by returning as soon as possible to as normal a routine as we can arrange, allowing their days and life to have structure. If old routines are painful, we can develop new ones. Keeping busy is a blessing for siblings, whether in school activities, hobbies or social engagements.

Understanding that siblings grieve differently than we parents do helps us as they jump from one activity to another. They grieve in spurts; they can be crying their eyes out one minute and the next minutes be talking on the phone, watching a movie, going on a bike ride, listening to loud music, or playing with friends. Many siblings rely on friends to be their faithful listeners, and sometimes this is hard for us parents to accept. But it's part of sibling grief. It might be easier for our children to talk to a friend or even another trusted adult rather than to us. In fact, many times they are afraid of adding to our pain, so we should just be grateful they are talking to someone.

We might encourage journal writing, or drawing for younger children, encouraging them to pour out their hearts on paper, releasing the feelings and thoughts that haunt them, saying the things they wish they had said or that need to be said now. We can share helpful books, poems and articles on grief issues. Anything that touches our heart might move theirs as well, providing them moments of welcome comfort. Grief support books in the local library (the 155.937 section of both adult and children departments) can lead them to a treasure of inspiring information, moving stories, and touching poetry.

Another big help to siblings can be a family pet. We called our family dog, Mickey, the backbone of the family after the deaths of our children because he got us up, made us walk around the block, forced us to open the refrigerator, cuddled with us on the sofa, and snuggled with us in bed. He ministered to each one of us individually, taking turns keeping each of us company. He brought noise and laughter into our home. His big brown eyes always announced, "I know you are hurting and I am here for you." His message was loud and clear. What a greeting he gave our daughter as he jumped out of the car window at the train station each time she returned from college. At home, he ran up the stairs with her to her bedroom, helping her unload her duffel bag, poking his nose inside and checking out all the contents. He never left her side and helped fill up that lonesome bedroom she had shared with Peggy. He teased her by trying to take over the bed, even trying to push her out of it. He made the house feel alive again and gave her someone to talk to, to hug, to pet, to laugh and cry with, and to tell her secrets to. No money could ever repay that dog for his gentle, caring therapy. He was the perfect remedy for a brokenhearted, lonesome little sister.

The roller coaster of grief can cause outbursts or episodes of acting out.

We all know grieving is not smooth sailing. The roller coaster of grief can cause outbursts or episodes of acting out. A sibling might try different ways of imitating the deceased brother or sister, make attempts to fill their shoes, show indifference to school or a job, or take unnecessary risks. We need to be patient, knowing very well what is causing the problem.

We might pray, light candles, or plan family rituals together to remember the sibling who has died. Children can be very creative in coming up with ways to keep the memory of their brother or sister alive. One sibling in our Compassionate Friends chapter completed a solo 3,500-mile bike ride, cycling coast to coast and raising $5,000 for our chapter in memory of his brother. Other siblings might choose favorite photos to display, design collages to hang, or create "brag books" to carry with them to keep a closeness to their sibling and perhaps to share their brother or sister with others. Our children might find comfort in wearing things that belonged to their sibling or immersing themselves in things dear to their brother or sister. Donning their siblings' tee-shirts, sweatshirts, bathrobes, jackets and jewelry, listening to their favorite CDs, using their sports equipment, computer or stereo, driving their car, or just lying on their bed can make them feel connected in a special way. Sometimes they simply put a favorite object under their pillow to keep a sense of closeness with the sibling they miss so much.

Appreciating a stepparent's grief

Society many times seems to ignore the relationship or minimize the pain a bereaved stepparent suffers. Even though the stepparent has established a loving relationship with the child, and in many cases raised the child, some people are hesitant to offer the same level of sympathy they give a birth parent. This situation is more complicated when one or both biological parents are remarried. Many times this scenario seems to leave the stepparent in limbo. People find it difficult to cross barriers of divorce and remarriage and offer consolation to three or four people. Sometimes they just don't know how to approach a stepparent, thinking they are "less" a parent or "not even" a parent.

Stepparents often are expected to be a tower of strength for their spouse, but they need to have their pain recognized too.

Stepparents might have spent less time living with their stepchildren than the biological parent did, but that doesn't mean they love them any less. They love their husband or wife, and their pain intensifies seeing the grief that has engulfed their spouse and disrupted their marriage. Stepparents might also try to be a buffer between their spouse and their spouse's "ex." Although they are grieving themselves, stepparents often are expected to be a tower of strength for their spouse, but they need to have their pain recognized too.

A remarried couple needs to be there for each other, showing the public they both loved their child and they both hurt. They stand together through the wake and funeral, welcoming support from friends and family. They do not cut out the other biological parent but try to respect that parent's feelings and needs. Sometimes this is difficult due to previous disagreements and circumstances, but it helps if those things can be put aside for this difficult time when everyone is in various stages of shock and numbness. Having two camps at the wake and funeral just adds to the pain and trauma. Acknowledging the grief of all parents and stepparents allows friends and family to feel comfortable offering sympathy to all involved. Although my children's father and I had our issues over the years, we did not bring them to the wake and funeral. Instead we worked together to survive the ordeal and honor our dead children. My present husband, Joe, and I invited him and all the relatives from both sides back to our home for a luncheon after each funeral. We all grieved together, which certainly helped our Annie.

If a widow or widower has remarried, there is obviously no other parent to include in decisions after the death of a child, but other family members—such as a grandmother, grandfather or sibling—might feel they should have more say about funeral arrangements or other issues because they have been in the picture longer than a stepparent. Trying to consider everyone's feelings in this time of sorrow helps to keep animosity and aggravation at a minimum when strength and energy are at their lowest and no one needs any added stress. Nothing is to be gained by hurting people who are already hurting.

A stepparent's grief needs to be recognized and acknowledged for his or her healing to begin. Often the stepparent becomes a tower of strength for the biological parent, who is bent in half and inconsolable. Then you might hear people say, "Now I know why God sent you Joe" or "How lucky you are to have Mary." The stepparent can offer love, support, listening ears, a hand to hold, a comforting embrace, an oasis of hope, all conveying the message "I am here to walk the journey with you." But stepparents also need exactly the same thing from others.

Realizing the twofold pain of grandparents

No one expects to outlive their own child, much less their grandchild. The natural order is reversed and spins their world upside down. This painful loss needs to be acknowledged by others to allow grandparents to have a healthy channel for expressing their grief and to experience the uplifting feeling of having a loving support system surround them. We bereaved parents can be the first ones to acknowledge the depth of grandparents' grief, leading the way for others to do the same.

Even though we are struggling to cope and survive the death of our child, we parents can make a big difference for our own parents, if we simply try to share with them what we are learning on our grief journey. Then they too can begin to create their "new normal" while learning how to help their hearts. As we accompany each other, we gently remind our parents that they need to take care of themselves first before they can help anyone else. Although they are eager to be there for us, it is important for them to realize that they need to address their own issues first.

We can share with them what is helping us: going at our own pace, figuring out the daily routine that eases our pain, doing the things that bring us some relief, allowing ourselves to cry when we feel like it, exercising regularly, eating nutritious foods, getting enough rest, reading inspirational books, journaling, joining a support group, and whatever else brings a smile or a momentary pause from the unrelenting pain. We can remind them to be patient and not to put themselves on an unrealistic timetable. As they achieve success with any of our suggestions they can become good role models for us, our remaining children, and other relatives who are hurting too. Once they have a grip on their own grief they can be valuable assets to our entire extended family.

Grandparents can be filled with anger at the loss of their grandchild and consumed with guilt for not having been able to prevent the death. They would offer to swap places in a minute if they could. They can be haunted by the thought "It should have been me" and by the memories of past losses that this death triggers. It helps if they read about the grief process so they can understand the roller-coaster pattern and be prepared for the ups and downs that are part of mourning.

We can share poignant articles and books with our parents that have offered us positive thoughts or go together to the library or bookstore in search of new materials. We can share subscriptions to magazines for the bereaved. We can sign up together for bereavement seminars and conferences, choosing the workshops that meet each of our needs. We can attend with them various holiday programs, prayer services, or special religious services for the bereaved. We can light candles or recite the rosary as a family. We can do acts of kindness, establish a scholarship, begin a foundation, or do volunteer work as a team with them in memory of our child, their grandchild. We can visit the cemetery together, plant a garden together, or just share memories with one another. We can provide a highlight to a grandparent's day with a phone call, an e-mail or a spur-of-the-moment cup of tea or coffee together. Simple things can open doors to their heart—letting good thoughts in and painful grief out.

Simple things can open doors to their heart—letting good thoughts in and painful grief out.

As grandparents regain some energy and strength, they can feel the reward of reaching out more to us and actually helping us. They can talk about their grandchild, be loving listeners, remember special days such as birthdays and anniversaries, help develop some new meaningful family rituals, and spend extra time with their other grandchildren, who are hurting too. They can help run errands, do laundry, cook meals, carpool and baby-sit. They can provide lots of hugs and listening ears. Bonding can become very strong when grandparents are able to both give and receive help sharing the family sorrow. It's kind of a two-way street. We can "rescue" our parents, who grieve the loss of their grand-child, simply by including them on our journey.

Supporting classmates and friends in their grief

If our child was of school age or older, he or she probably accumulated a circle of friends and classmates. Friends feel the loss of our child, too, and are shaken up by having to deal with their own mortality, which our child's death has forced them to face. Attending the wake and funeral make the death very real and can be very painful for them. It might be their first experience with the death of someone close to them. They offer their condolences to us and to our family, but because they are not family no one seems to acknowledge the grief that is heavy on their hearts.

Most people don't realize the depth of the pain the classmates and friends are experiencing or the thoughts that are haunting them, such as: *Who will be next? This could happen to me!* Classmates and friends need to talk, to share stories, to cry, to learn about the grief process—the same things we need. Some schools act quickly, offering crisis counseling to groups and individuals upon request. They are aware that it is not healthy for classmates to stuff feelings of grief down inside. This counseling can be during class periods, lunch or in evening hours. However, not all school counselors are trained in handling bereavement, so some programs are better than others. Sometimes professional individual counseling or support groups are available through local agencies or hospitals and might be suggested by school counselors, teachers, clergy or concerned friends. These support groups are usually professionally led and charge no fee; individual counseling at some agencies might have a charge, usually based on a sliding scale.

An understanding teacher can do wonders by acknowledging the pain of grieving students and giving them support.

Some good teachers are able to address the loss and provide activities or assignments that help classmates deal with their grief rather than ignore it. Writing letters or drawing pictures or cards to send the bereaved family, writing an article for the school paper, creating a memorial program, planting a tree, designing a memory booklet, dedicating a school event to the deceased friend or just spending time listening to classmates share their memories in an open classroom forum—all are ways of expressing feelings and emotions that need to be voiced. There are also many beautiful books and videos teachers and librarians can suggest that can open the heart to healing. An understanding teacher can do wonders by acknowledging the pain of grieving students and giving them support.

When I taught third grade (and before my own children had died), one of my students was killed crossing the street in front of the school. The little boy was well loved and had endeared himself to everybody because of the unique ways he handled his reading problems. I asked each student in his class to write a sentence about him. As we stood out on the school front lawn surrounding the tree we were planting in his memory, each one read his touching thought. There were many smiles and grins remembering his playful nature and the fine boy he was. We sang "Edelweiss," (little white flower), since he had just received his First Communion the week before, and we changed the words to echo his personality. It was a beautiful tribute and helped his classmates share their feelings. Little did I realize how much that ceremony touched those young lives. The children's parents went out of their way to thank me for handling the situation in such a loving, comforting way. Rituals help keep memories alive and bring a sense of comfort to the aching heart.

My son was a lifeguard the summer he died and the five summers before. He swam, raced, surfed and enjoyed the carefree friendship of the other lifeguards, mostly college students like himself. These young men and women were the honorary pallbearers at his funeral, and their faces reflected their stunned feelings of disbelief: *How could this 6'3" guy, in perfect physical condition, a champion swimmer, the life of the party, who was just joking and talking with me, be dead?* My daughter's sorority sisters, a close clan who shared all the trials and tribulations of college life, showed the same disbelief when Peggy's precious young life was snuffed out. Their voices were lowered, their eyes were wet with tears, and their lives were forever changed. Losing a dear friend is a jolt that leaves an impact. They suffer a loss of innocence as their lives take a hit they never imagined could happen.

Sometimes a dead child's friends become faithful visitors to the bereaved parents, and we welcome them into our life. They are a living reminder that our child is not erased from people's memory, and that brings a sense of joy to our heart. They help us laugh and feel loved and cared about. When we invite them to our home or greet them on a spur-of-the-moment visit, we help them too. It's another two-way street—we validate their grief as they attempt to console us. They need to talk, tell their stories, share their memories, mention their fears, and feel their sorrow in order to successfully process their grief. They need us almost as much as we need them. Their presence fills a void for us, and our presence in their life is a link for them to the friend they lost.

We try to share some of our wisdom with them, or at least what we have learned so far. We are grateful for their visits. I can still see my kids' friends bringing me Mother's Day plants and Christmas poinsettias; attending special Masses honoring birthdays and anniversaries; sending cards; or dropping by for a quick hug. Now I run into them pushing a baby stroller in a supermarket, jogging by our house, dancing at weddings. As life goes on and new interests and responsibilities come along, their visits have become less frequent or have ended altogether, but Joe and I have given them our silent blessing, glad that their lives are moving forward and that we were instrumental in helping them on that journey.

This is my comfort in my distress,
that your promise gives me life.

Psalm 119:50

Responding to a Special Love

You have turned my mourning into dancing; you have taken off my sackcloth and clothed me with joy, so that my soul may praise you and not be silent.
Psalm 30:11

Welcoming the comfort of solitude

When we're grieving the death of a child, we seem to do a lot of thinking. All the "if onlys" and "should have dones" seem to haunt us. Memories surround us. Wishes play havoc with us.

Sometimes just being able to stand back and explore all our jumbled feelings is a way to help our heart. It is not selfish but wise to take time out for ourselves to ponder all the things that assault our mind and cause us stress. Solitude is a way to help us understand ourselves, to discover our needs, to name our fears, and to figure out a plan to address them. We need to take some time alone to think, cry, do nothing, pray, meditate, draw, stare at the TV or write in a journal. Time spent alone can help us cope and heal.

Many of us are so tied into nurturing others, such as our spouse and remaining children, that we forget to make ourselves a priority. We get caught up in all life's happenings and fail to insure time for our own needs. After Peggy's and Denis' deaths, I often found special time to "collapse" each evening. I would relax, read, or just ponder what I had read. It was a time of day when I was exhausted and welcomed some quiet time. As much as I used to enjoy reading bestsellers before my children died, they no longer interested me. Instead I spent hours reading every support book I could lay my hands on. How grateful I was for their wisdom and insights. It was like having a guardian angel pointing me in the right direction—and maybe it was! At the time I didn't realize how much help it was to create a special time like that for myself each day. But it was the ritual—the making time for myself, the learning experience, the trying new ideas, the pondering my own thoughts—that led me out of the Valley of the Shadow. Figuring out how to include my Peggy and Denis in my present life, how to keep remembering their looks, their voices, their touch, their personalities, how to reweave our family fabric—all of that happened in the time I made for myself.

Most of us bereaved parents examine everything we are doing and ask ourselves, "Is this important?" We narrow our list of priorities. We note activities we can do or will try to do. We avoid useless, frivolous ones and skip the trivial things. We learn to conserve our energy and to avoid things that cause stress. We value loving listeners and welcome a loving support system. We recognize the people who nurture us through our grief, and we dismiss those who try to hurry us along or attempt to take our grief away from us. Quietly meditating on all these topics stirs up a lot of baggage, which we need time to sort out. We go slowly and try to work through one issue at a time in the holy darkness of our grief. Whenever we learn something about ourselves, we are another step ahead on our path to healing.

Solitude can be healing, but we must be careful to avoid isolation.

Solitude can be healing, but we must be careful to avoid isolation. Solitude is taking time out; isolation is going away. When we isolate ourselves, we cut ourselves off from others and their caring and objectivity. We need them for balance in our thinking. We need them around as loving listeners. Taking time out for ourselves helps, but cutting ourselves off from others is how we deepen our wounds and prolong our healing.

Sometimes just the quiet is what our heart needs—kind of a time to catch our breath. In the silence of our soul God waits for us. We can turn within and find that God gently reassures us that we have an unlimited supply of strength and courage. In the silence, God is there. As we let the silence embrace us, we can feel God's infinite love and power. We can listen as God speaks to us. This is a kind of listening beyond what ears can hear. We just listen, for God knows what is on our heart and mind. He fills us with words of assurance, direction, and whatever else we need to hear.

In our solitude some of us like to write about what we are feeling at the time; some, like me, like to read; some like to listen to music; some need time to think about sticky issues that nag us; some need to search for meaning in the loss; and some simply enjoy the refuge of prayer or poetry.

Taking time to meditate can have its positive rewards. We might develop a stronger faith, become more compassionate and caring, or live life more fully because of our increased awareness of its preciousness and fragility. We can learn to enjoy life's daily journey instead of always waiting for some planned future destination, which we may never reach. Through meditation we can discover purpose and meaning for our life, and that is crucial in helping us resolve our grief.

Starting the day with meditation can make us more aware of God's presence throughout the routine and challenge of the day. Our hearts are open for discovery. How wonderful to fill them with God's wisdom, which guides us; his inspiration, which encourages us; and his very Spirit, which enlivens us. Every day we are aware that his care is a blessing in our life.

Reviving our spirit through music

The healing power of music is another source of revitalization for our damaged spirit. It could be the touching lyrics or the lingering melody that offers solace to our wounded heart. The words of some songs speak volumes to our heart—saying exactly what we are thinking, expressing out loud what we want to say—whether it's pop music, rock 'n' roll, country-western, gospel or church hymn. Each song answers a need that is screaming from our heart.

For Sunday Mass and special sacramental celebrations our family always loved the guitar groups and their musical renditions of our favorite songs. For my children's funerals, I invited a guitarist/vocalist who had stolen our hearts at a wedding only two weeks earlier. Through his gift of "singing in the Spirit," our hearts were lifted and embraced by the voices of the entire congregation as they sang each song with gusto. He thoughtfully presented me with a tape of his inspiring religious songs, which included "Come Lord Jesus," a song he composed that was the meditation song at my children's funerals. I played that tape a hundred times a day, imploring the Lord Jesus to "fill my soul, make me whole, help me to stand, I'll fear no harm, I am secure in your arms." No matter what I was doing—cooking, cleaning, dusting, vacuuming—that music was medicine for my heart. The vision of the Lord holding me tightly in his arms did wonders for me. The song actually made me smile and feel a very special connection with my children. Playing it again and again, I wore the tape out. (I was lucky that Ernie, the singer/composer, was able to send me a second one.) I could have driven my husband out of the house with the constant playing of those songs, but he seemed to understand my needs. The melodies, the words, the message, the vision—all mingled to soothe my aching heart.

At a Compassionate Friends meeting when I asked for suggestions of songs bereaved parents found comforting, hands shot up and voices called out a multitude of song titles: "Precious Child," "Amazing Grace," "Fly," "Tears in Heaven," "Forever Young," "Wind Beneath My Wings," "The Rose," "Angels Among Us," "My Heart Will Go On," "The Dance," "I Will Remember You," "To Where You Are," and more. It was amazing that each of us had found a different musical tonic for our soul. How wonderful that there are so many poignant songs ready to minister to our hearts! Some found instrumental and classical music a balm for their wounds, a perfect companion in their quiet time, taking the edge off their loneliness and longing for their child, filling an empty space in their heart.

In church, many of us found favorite hymns that invited us to lean on their healing words: "Shepherd Me, O God," repeating the soothing words of the 23rd Psalm; "All I Ask of You," reminding us to "forever remember me as loving you;" "On Eagle's Wings," telling us we will be held "in the palm of his hand;" and "Be Not Afraid," counseling us that "I will give you rest." Each has its own tender and powerful heartfelt message for us. The words of "Here I Am, Lord" bring tears to my eyes every time I hear them, because they remind me so poignantly of my Peggy. "Here I Am, Lord" was the inscription on the cover of her funeral Mass booklet, and my mind pictures her in her exuberance announcing at the pearly gates, "Here I Am, Lord!" To this day that song deeply touches my soul. If we find some words we identify with, repeating them over and over again can bring a sense of contentment and joy to our heart.

How grateful I am to recapture those memorable moments of musical delight.

Some of our children's favorite tapes or CDs can keep memories alive for us, remembering how much our children enjoyed certain artists, groups and favorite songs. Listening to the Beatles, the Grateful Dead, the Beach Boys, the Clancy Brothers, the theme songs from school sports nights, music from favorite movies such as *The Sound of Music*, *The Wizard of Oz* and *Grease*, and old-time Christmas carols helps me remember happy times and the delight music has always been for our family. I cannot hear Charlie Daniels' "The Devil Went Down to Georgia" without grinning from ear to ear imagining Denis as a teenager singing that foot-stomping song loud and clear each morning as he was getting ready for school; or the musical strains of Phil Collins' hits of the 1980s, which Peggy loved to sing, knowing every single word; or the sounds of the booming West Point Marching Band, which the kids would blast on the stereo as a joke when they knew someone wanted to sleep late. I can smile, laugh, shed a tear and reminisce listening to these reminders of life with Peggy and Denis. How grateful I am to recapture those memorable moments of musical delight.

Some bereaved parents have found solace singing in a church or community choir. Singing their hearts out, they find a physical and emotional outlet that provides some structure and fills many hours with something they actually enjoy. Singing for local hospitals, nursing homes and senior citizen centers offers them a way to reach out to others, which is healing in itself. Seeing frail bodies, lonesome souls and people enduring hardships even prompts many bereaved parents to count blessings they had refused to acknowledge or had taken for granted up to this point. Some share their singing talent with schoolchildren and Sunday school classes, helping them prepare for seasonal concerts and special holiday programs. For bereaved parents, just keeping busy, getting out of the house, dealing with other people, memorizing new words and learning new arrangements teaches them that even though the world is full of suffering, it is full also of the overcoming of sorrow and loss.

There is no one way to grieve, even though many people think there is.

Not everyone responds to the healing power of music. Some parents could not even think of turning on the radio or playing a CD, much less attending a concert. It is too painful for them to allow those happy sounds to enter their daily routine. They need a different outlet for their grief, and they will discover one that fits their yearnings. There is no one way to grieve, even though many people think there is. I remember driving to a bereavement conference with a car full of bereaved mothers. I turned on the car radio, which was normal for me. Instantly one of the moms asked me to turn it off, saying she could not bear to listen to music. As I turned off the radio I was saddened that my friend wasn't able to experience the warm embrace of music's melody and words, which can make my heart feel like it is wrapped in velvet. It is my salvation on so many days—filling me with the rhythm of life, reverberating as an affirmation of renewal and healing throughout my body.

Relishing nature's beauty

Simple things like a single rose, a towering sunflower, or a "loves-me, loves-me-not" daisy can open our eyes and hearts to a world that keeps going even though our child has died. Quiet inviting places, such as a peaceful lake, a scenic mountainside, or a secluded beach, might offer us the perfect setting to find solitude or family togetherness to soothe us in our grief. It could be a star-kissed sky, a brilliant moon, a radiant sun, swirling snowflakes, or the patter of raindrops that offers hope to our heart. Nature's beauty comes in many shapes and sizes, offering us a connection to the universe that many of us might have been ignoring. Snow-capped mountains, swaying palm trees, crashing waves, lush meadows, shady hiking trails, crystal-clear waters and splashing waterfalls are magnetic in their sheer beauty. They touch our soul, that center of our spirituality, reminding us that we are part of a greater universe. Nature's beauty can awaken feelings that have been dormant for a while and make us feel alive again—connected in some special way to our child who is no longer physically present. Nature's beauty subtly reminds us there is a power greater than ourselves in the universe. It helps us recognize that change and endings are the natural order of things. Relishing nature's beauty can be a beginning in establishing new connections with those around us; with our child, who seems so far away from us; and with our God, who might seem distant and remote in our grief. Nature puts things in perspective. Going outdoors can be powerful therapy for us.

Flowers seem especially magical the way they can lift spirits—whether it's a single bud, a bouquet, or a full flowerpot or garden. Their unique beauty and array of colors and fragrances comfort us. One bereaved mother said: "I treat myself to a bouquet each week from the market. I tell myself it is a gift from my daughter, put it right on the kitchen table, and smile every time I gaze at it. It reminds me of the wildflowers she used to pick as a child and present so proudly to me."

One Christmas my sister-in-law gave me a box containing a flowerpot, a bag of soil, an amaryllis bulb, and instructions on how to plant it to grow indoors. It was the most amazing flower, growing inches every day. It grew so fast that my husband began taking daily pictures of it, like he was going to catch it growing on film. Each morning we were thrilled with the progress of the plant, and we were ecstatic when it burst into bloom with huge red petals in a matter of days. All of a sudden another stem popped up through the soil, grew rapidly in height, and soon we had a second big red flower. That plant mesmerized us, became the center of attention in our home, and kept us engaged for weeks. We were like two little kids with our favorite toy. The amaryllis gave us hours of nurturing time, photography time and laughter time.

Joe and I also planted a special garden at our home in memory of our children. Carefully choosing the flowers, arranging them by height and color, feeding and watering them, and whacking weeds that dared to enter this sacred spot brought hours of planning, digging, nurturing and joy to this bereaved mother's heart. Adding more rosebushes and assorted seasonal flowers to the garden each year, and enjoying the bountiful bouquets cut from it, keep Peggy's and Denis' presence very near. Installing boy and girl figurines, a watchful garden angel, an inviting butterfly birdhouse, a splashing birdbath and a welcoming St. Francis statue enhanced this labor of love. The garden offered a million ways to make me smile at nature's beauty as I watched the flowers grow and the birds, butterflies and squirrels congregate there, enjoying my green-thumb efforts. Even the raccoons and bunnies ran through occasionally to check out the garden. I have planted many a garden in my day, but I don't remember one ever connecting my heart to life and growth and the greater universe like this garden has. As the garden grew, so did my appreciation of life's cycle and the connection with my God, the creator of it all.

I also enjoyed many hours of renewal at the ocean beach. I was afraid to visit it in that first year, thinking it would be too painful because of all the memories of happy family times there. But I was pleasantly surprised. The ebb and flow of tides, the powerful waves, the beautiful whitecaps echoing nature's beauty refueled me and refreshed my soul, allowing me to rejoice in my memories. Many bereaved parents say that walking the beach is great therapy. As you walk, you seem to empty your heart of the bitter feelings of anger, guilt, anxiety and depression and instead fill it with a sweet sense of calm.

All of us welcome different things in nature to fill the emptiness of our heart. Twinkling stars, glorious rainbows, breathtaking sunrises and all the other wonders of nature invite us to feel the loving embrace of our God, the creator and sustainer of life. Nature reminds us that he is with us at all times and in all places, even in our grief.

Finding renewal in a hobby

Days that seem long and empty without any delight for our spirit may be calling us to get immersed in an activity that fills some hours with peace, gives meaning to our day, and provides an outlet for our feelings and emotions. We might seek the comfort of an old hobby that used to hold our interest and passion, such as piano playing, card games, crocheting, sewing, carpentry, gardening, stamp collecting, bird watching, painting or cooking. Or we might wish to find a new outlet for our creativity and emotions, such as studying a foreign language, making crafts, learning calligraphy, investigating digital photography, writing poetry, tracing genealogy, making furniture, baking bread, wallpapering, learning bird calls, painting portraits, studying opera, compiling family photographs for video production, taking computer courses, or programming a Palm Pilot. Whatever sparks our interest is worth checking out. As the old proverb says, "An idle mind is the devil's workshop," and for bereaved parents the devil's name is Depression.

We all need one hobby to open the door for our heart—to let some fresh air in, to invite us to feel alive again.

Some of us find solace in continuing a hobby our child relished. It could be trading baseball cards, playing computer games, shooting photography, riding a dirt bike—the list is endless. Whatever your choice, it will bring times of relaxation and real moments of peace in the life you are trying to reorganize. We all need one hobby to open the door for our heart—to let some fresh air in, to invite us to feel alive again.

In those early days of grief I found pleasure in collecting angels, a few for myself but mostly to give to others to remind them of Peggy and Denis. This hobby became a passion that gave me energy and made me smile as I inscribed each of the heavenly messengers in memory of my children. The hobby filled hours of my evenings after work and dinner and made weekends fly by. Then I discovered the comfort of making flowered wreaths, enjoying the beauty of the wide variety of silk flowers and colorful ribbons available. (I even took orders from friends in our support group who were delighted to adorn their child's grave with one of my wreaths. This was one of our first fund-raisers for our Compassionate Friends chapter. By making the wreaths I kept happily busy and added a few dollars to our chapter's treasury, enabling us to expand our tiny lending library.)

Just practicing difficult measures let my mind escape into the serenity of music.

I also rediscovered an old hobby —playing the piano—that had been dormant for a while. It offered another outlet that brought a sense of peace to my heart. Playing the family favorites and the ones the children had joined in on with their flutes and clarinet brought back a lot of soothing memories. Just practicing difficult measures over and over let my mind escape into the serenity of music. Pounding those keys loudly or touching them ever so softly was an outlet echoing the mood swings of my heart.

One dad took computer courses and learned to convert his family pictures into booklets he could give to friends and relatives as keepsakes. He spent days and many tears choosing just the right pictures that touched his heart. Others have copied their children's poetry and writings; they're so grateful to have those precious words on paper and are thrilled to share them with relatives and friends.

Another mom and dad spent time arranging their 24-year-old son's artwork and sculpture collections for art shows held at their son's college, their town library, their local high school art department, and the fine arts studio at the state university. A lot of work went into publicity, transporting the pieces to each place, setting up the display, and being present to chat with visitors to the exhibits. The same family adopted a town-owned lot, known as a "pocket park," in their community in memory of that son, who had died in an auto accident. The parents, their four remaining children and their spouses, and all the grandchildren decorate the huge tree in the center of the park at Christmastime. They have a tree-lighting ceremony and a visit from Santa there each year, welcoming the entire community to the festivities. The dad feels connected to his son as he maintains the flowers and shrubbery, weeding and watering faithfully all year. The mom hosts an annual Mother's Day plant sale at the site, raising money for the local garden club in her son's name. The family has the joy of knowing a whole town remembers their son and annually celebrates with them. These hobbies brought smiles, lighter hearts, and even some new friends. (I renewed my friendship with this family; I had taught their son in third grade 16 years earlier, and I have enjoyed all the ways they have remembered him and shared him. It helped my heart, too.)

Another bereaved father, whose son took his own life, found hours of pleasurable escape retreating into the garage workshop he had built and using his carpentry skills to make furniture for and special craft pieces as gifts for his family and friends. Concentrating on patterns and dimensions, materials to be used, and bric-a-brac to be added, he whiled away hours while getting his mind thoroughly involved in his projects.

Another parent diligently worked on producing an inspirational CD in memory of his son, composing new melodies and choosing some favorite old ones. He couldn't wait to get to his makeshift home studio each day to complete the labor of love. Making the final cut, selecting the packaging, writing the dedication, and choosing photos for the CD jacket gave him the joy of doing something he knew his son would have loved.

One mom discovered a motivational tape produced by her son, who had been killed by a drunk driver. She combined his actual words on the tape with a song she wrote, "The Gifts of Life and Love," to create a CD educating the public about offering others a "second chance to live" by saying yes to organ donation.

A dad spent the whole first year after his teenage daughter's death from a skiing accident designing the most beautiful tombstone for her. He spent hours researching granite selections, designs and leading sculptors for cemetery monuments. He channeled his pain into producing a lasting memorial for his precious daughter, making sure future generations would remember her.

Within each of us there is a fountain of divine ideas. By tuning in to that inner voice in us, we can tap into these ideas and find novel ways to refresh ourselves. We can invite the creativity of the Spirit to pour into our activities. Then sparks of divine ideas can give renewed life to our projects. Sometimes we might be surprised to find that a hobby we chose for relaxation leads us to a new career or helps us improve our health. I believe these unexpected blessings are the results of God's presence working through people and events in our life to bring about greater good for us and through us.

Rejuvenating ourselves through physical activity

The more support books we read, the more we discover people raving about the benefits of physical activity as a help overcoming grief. According to research, exercise provides a welcome release for the emotions and feelings that overwhelm us after the death of our child. It might be hard for us to get out of our chair or bed or to even think of leaving the house, but finding a physical way to shed some of the frustration and anger that accompanies loss is a giant step on our grief journey. All kinds of physical activities are available to answer our need to reduce tension and anxiety, express aggression, and relieve depression.

Although some parents find their salvation in pursuing a sport or activity they loved before their child died, or even one they enjoyed with their child, others discover that some of their favorite old pastimes are just too painful to even consider. This could be because of all the memories involved or because of guilt from not having spent enough time with their child. Sometimes parents simply feel that they should not be having anything resembling fun when society feels they should be in mourning. But whether it's an old sport or activity or one brand new to us, we don't have to wait for others to give us permission to pursue it. We can allow ourselves to grieve our own way, finding the things that help us deal with our deep grief, knowing they will lead us to healing. We learn to overcome our pain in ways that bring us comfort, even if they don't meet society's expectations.

Even if we do something as simple as walking around the block, that's a beginning. It gets us to focus on something besides the death of our child. Walking enables us to commune with nature, meditate, listen to encouraging tapes and CDs, get energized, enjoy a sunrise or sunset, wave to a neighbor or just walk our dog. It's a first step outside of ourselves.

Many find jogging an answer to their prayers. It gets them outside, breathing fresh air, feeling the exhilaration of the process, and maybe even feeling pain from the effort. But it's a different kind of pain than our grief—almost a welcome replacement pain!

Others return to a sport they love, hoping that playing tennis, basketball or racquetball will bring moments of relief. They rely on that sport to get them out of the house and moving, or to get them tired enough to get a good night's sleep. (We all know how many times we lay awake or wake up during the night and see our child's face smack in front of us—so clearly we can almost reach out and touch it, as we wish we could! So many of us walk the floors at night unable to fall asleep; we would welcome an activity that might gift us with some precious hours of sleep.)

Being able to hit something with all our might lets out a lot of the anger we have accumulated. Being angry is part of the grief process. We can't avoid the emotion; we have to work through it, even if we are of the mindset that nice people don't get angry. There is something very therapeutic about being able to hit, swing, pound or strike an object as hard as we can. We can even cry as we are doing it and feel the double blessed

> *There is something very therapeutic about being able to hit, swing, pound or strike an object as hard as we can.*

release of both tears and tension.

Some of us find the refuge of golf a saving grace in our lives, offering hours of solace from the heart-wrenching agony we are enduring. Walking the course, addressing that ball, and deciding what club to use can give a respite from the sadness and grief that are part of our every day. Attempting a friendly golf game or just hitting a bucket of balls at a driving range can jump start an aching heart back into the rhythm of life again, offering us a few pain-free moments.

Many bereaved parents sing the praises of running to the gym when they are having a bad day. How glad they are to have a place where they can run on a treadmill, challenge a Stairmaster, or choose another challenging exercise machine to free them for a while from the anxiety and depression that are swallowing them up. The relief they experience from the physical activity and the unloading of a heavy burden empowers them to know that healing is possible and that they have taken a step in that direction.

Through physical activity together, one couple seemed to exhaust their raw grief.

One couple walked the Appalachian Trail—2,100 miles from Georgia to Maine, an experience that restored their spirits. After losing their child in a plane crash they needed something that was fully physical, time-consuming and challenging. They limped, nursed blisters, laughed, cried, sang, collapsed, and suffered sunburn, pebbles in the shoes, scrapes, bruises and rain-soaked clothing, but they endured the hardships, and their spirits soared as they accomplished the tough grind they had set for themselves. They grieved out loud, having the freedom to yell, scream, whistle, sing—telling each other and the world how they really felt. Through physical activity together, they seemed to exhaust their raw grief.

One bereaved father learned the wonders of karate. It answered his needs to vent his frustration and find a release from the all-consuming pain. He could scream, shout, kick and punch, alleviating some of the feelings of anger and guilt that overwhelmed him since the death of his only son in a car accident. Never did he realize how many emotions he had stuffed down inside himself until he began his karate lessons. How thrilled his wife was to have him yelling and shouting at someone else! How lucky he felt to unload the crippling emotions and to begin the work of healing.

Spending hours fishing or boating can be another escape from our inner turmoil, giving us a change of surroundings and something to focus on. Bike riding invites us to enjoy new scenery, feel the breeze in our face, soak up some sunshine, or have special time with our spouse or remaining children. It also can offer us a kind of instant get-away when we just need to get out of the house and leave our problems behind. In colder weather, ice skating, hockey, skiing, sledding or snowboarding can come to our aid if these are sports we can handle. Otherwise, we might just get some relief from making a snowman, pushing a snow blower or making hot cocoa for the ice skaters in our family. Anything that gets our mind off our suffering and invites our bodies to get activated helps us move forward with our grieving. Some bereaved parents pursue the serenity of yoga, the exercise of aerobics or the routine of dance classes to keep their minds and bodies focused on sequenced steps, hoping to keep sad thoughts at bay for a few moments.

Heartfelt moments might be our reward for coaching children's teams—football, baseball, soccer, basketball, lacrosse and the like—especially if it's a sport our child pursued with vigor. Doing it in memory of our son or daughter is a great motivator and can make us feel a powerful link with our deceased child. One dad organized a town lacrosse league in memory of his son, who had died from a brain tumor at 22 and had enjoyed lacrosse with a passion. To keep his son's memory alive and to promote his keen love of the sport, this dad introduced hundreds of children to the sport and made sure every child learned the game and got a chance to play. He spent hours taking care of all the paperwork and then plunged into the demanding coach's role, feeling his son's healing presence, laughter and cheering at the practices and games.

Realizing that something good comes from our loss, knowing that our children would be applauding our decision to carry on their favorite sport, and being involved with hours of passionate work can be real lifts for our heart.

If we don't have the energy, skills or desire to participate in a sport, or if our age or health prevents it, we might find relaxation and a change of pace by watching a football, basketball or baseball game, a tennis match, an ice skating competition or a round of golf on TV. Just being distracted from our grief is a step in the right direction. As I've watched the U.S. Open tennis tournament each summer here in New York, my heart has felt the presence of my Peggy and Denis as I recall the many happy memories of us all cheering wildly for Jimmy Connors, howling at the hilarious antics of John McEnroe and being enchanted with the charm and talent of Chris Evert.

Feeling the healing power of a pet

I can't give enough good reasons for having a pet when you are grieving. When you're feeling down, melancholy, depressed or ready to cry at the drop of a hat, the unconditional love of a pet can be the pick-me-up you need to bring a smile to your face and a measure of comfort to your broken heart. The simple presence, the big eyes that seem to say "I understand," the friendly antics, and just knowing they won't offer you advice can do wonders for your spirit. Whether it's a dog, cat, bird or other animal that captures your heart, no money could ever repay pets for their gentle, caring therapy when you feel so vulnerable.

It turned out to be fortunate for our family that I had given in when Denis begged for a black Labrador retriever for his 16th birthday. We went to the North Shore Animal League, where Denis chose a black Lab and German shepherd mix that looked exactly like a full-pedigree black lab. He named him Michelob, which quickly shortened to "Mickey," and he became the buddy and confidant of my three teenagers, who bared their souls to him. Playing Frisbee with Denis, baking cookies with Peggy, getting treats from Annie, he befriended each in a different way and became a sounding board for the ups and downs of their teenage years.

Five years later, when Peggy and Denis died, Mickey became the healing backbone of our family, nurturing us tenderly and completely. We are thankful to him for doing things to make us laugh, for getting us out to exercise a few times a day, for licking away our tears, and for snuggling on the sofa or in bed with us. Mickey got us out of bed in the morning, led us to the back door, walked us gently around the block while listening to all our woes, let us cry our hearts out, and never told anybody our secrets.

Petting him, stroking his furry ears, or scratching his tummy gave us such peace.

He'd lie by the front door each day waiting for us to return from work. Even when we went on trips he sensed the exact time of our arrival home and would be waiting to greet us wildly at the front door. When Annie wasn't around he'd stealthily climb onto our bed and creep in between Joe and me, falling sound asleep on the electric blanket he loved. I couldn't wake up and not smile, even when visions of Peggy and Denis haunted my soul. Petting him, stroking his furry ears, or scratching his tummy gave us such peace. We couldn't open the refrigerator without his being right there next to us, showing up from out of nowhere!

As I cooked dinner he'd be under my feet; as I ironed he curled up under the ironing board; as I did the laundry he marched up and down the cellar stairs with me. As I unpacked the groceries he stuck his head in each bag—and many times strutted around the kitchen with the paper bag on his head! How could I not laugh? Whenever I felt sad his smile made me feel good all over. And yes, dogs *do* smile.

We all agreed that Mickey had the fastest tongue in the East. Hors d'oeuvres were open season, and raw steaks for barbecuing had to be guarded carefully. Keeping us busy, he nurtured us through the rough days and added a sparkle and zest to our life. If we were sick in bed, he'd climb right in with us and never leave our side, even if we were burning up with fever. He always made us feel better. That's why we called him our "head nurse."

As I faithfully walked him each day I'd look up to heaven and whisper gratefully to Denis, "Thanks for Mickey. He makes my heart sing!" As Mickey approached 14, a little slower and a tad stiffer, no longer able to leap onto the sofa or bed but still as lovable as ever, Joe and I wondered, "What will we do if something happens to Mickey? Will we get another dog? Should we get one before Mickey joins Peggy and Denis, or should we be just free as birds and have no dog at all?"

Before we could reach a decision, the phone rang and my cousin told us he needed to find a home for a friend's two-year-old pedigree black Lab. "Would you like to have him?" he said. I happily said to my husband: "Do you think God is talking to us?" Four days later 96-pound Max joined our family and rejuvenated his new "brother," Mickey. Becoming instant friends, they enjoyed strolling around the dining room table together, swapping their bowls of puppy kibble and mushy senior food, whispering in each other's ears, sunbathing together on the deck, and riding in the back seat of the car together. They certainly added noise and laughter to our day.

It was a wonderful year and a half until our dear little Mickey's hind legs couldn't match his strong heart. Tearfully, we bid a tender farewell to our gentle 15-year-old caretaker and tightly hugged his protégé—just a few weeks before the 10th anniversaries of Peggy's and Denis' deaths. What a great anniversary present for them, I thought, and sharing Mickey with them helped me accept his death. His special link with our grief did not seem broken, but extended and shared.

Pets get under your skin and provide healthy nurturing. Relaxing with them, petting them, smiling at them and their routines, talking to them, enjoying their presence, feeding them, and feeling needed all contribute to our healing. They become beloved friends and family members, adding sunshine to our days and a new heartfelt dimension to our life.

The Lord is near to the brokenhearted,
and saves the crushed in spirit.

Psalm 34:18

Singing Their Song

O my strength, I will sing praises to you, for you O God,
are my fortress, the God who shows me steadfast love.
                                                    Psalm 59:17

Sharing their possessions

A lament often heard from bereaved parents is, *What do I do*
with my child's things? It is hard enough to lose a child, but to
have to go through all their possessions is simply gut wrench-
ing. Getting it through our head and heart that our child is no
longer here is such a huge and awful task that it can't be done
quickly. It's slow and painful work, accomplished a day and a
memory at a time. Everywhere we turn we are surrounded with
reminders of our child—clothes, toys, games, tapes, videos,
sports equipment, trophies, jewelry, posters, books, papers,
photographs and favorite foods. We can't just walk away from
all the things that echo their name. Yet dealing with each pos-
session feels like getting kicked in the stomach again and again.
It takes our breath away. Going through drawer after drawer,
box upon box, desk, bookcase and closet is time-consuming,
heartbreaking, tearful work. It leaves us exhausted.

None of us wants our child erased, so we are not eager to
change his or her room in any way. We are careful not to throw
away the possessions they loved most—teddy bear, doll, ballet
slippers, baseball glove, books, posters or other prized items. We
cling to these reminders, sensing our child's essence and presence. Determined to never forget, we save things for ourselves
and for special people in our child's life.

But what do we do with them?

Contrary to what most people think, there is no need or
rush to empty out your child's room. It's hard to even enter that
room, knowing your child is not there and never will be again.
So listen to your heart. It will let you know when you are ready

or strong enough to face the grim task of sorting out your child's possessions.

First, you need to talk together as a family, sharing what is comfortable for each of you. You might not agree what to do with the possessions or even on a timetable for dealing with them. You might have to compromise on some issues. It's important to listen to everyone's thoughts and be respectful of one another's feelings, honoring the distinct relationship each of you had with the child.

Some of us just need more time to deal with the fact that our child will never again occupy that room.

Some family members might not want to change a thing, leaving the bed unmade, the sneakers on the floor, clothes thrown on the chair, the bulletin board loaded with notices. Others want to tidy up the room and leave it in pristine condition, making it almost like a shrine. Some might want to empty the room of all reminders of the child, thinking that will help them move on in their grief. Others want to close the door and declare the room off-limits. Many parents find ways to make the room a place where they can retreat and feel the presence of their child. In that special room they install their computer, use their exercise equipment, fold laundry, wrap packages, sew, iron or pursue hobbies. The room becomes a sacred space for them. Some just stretch out in the room, soaking in the atmosphere, while others find it the perfect spot for reading, meditating, writing letters or journaling. Some families choose to make it a guest room, den or library, and some rearrange the bedroom for another family member. Do you see how differently we all face this situation?

Some of us just need more time to deal with the fact that our child will never again occupy that room. We deserve the time to come to grips with the reality of our child's death. There is no award for hurrying, no prize for emptying the room out quickly. As many bereaved parents can attest, things done in haste can be bitterly regretted later.

Going through our child's things is an emotionally draining experience, best accomplished with a giant box of tissues on hand and a prayer on our lips. Everything we touch brings tears, all prompted by poignant memories. We will need a few days, maybe weeks, doing a little at a time, to accomplish this exhausting job.

Trying to be organized, we do a kind of triage with the possessions our child left behind. In one set of boxes we put the things we are not ready to part with. We save anything that makes our heart jump a beat: stuffed animals, photographs, watch, school ring, rosary, letters, cards, trophies, school papers, diplomas, yearbooks, favorite pieces of clothing. In another stack of boxes we save the things we want to share with our other children, relatives and friends as keepsakes: bracelets, necklaces, earrings, tee-shirts, bathrobe, sweaters, blanket, soccer ball, golf clubs, Blessed Mother statue—whatever we think would be a special keepsake for someone dear to our child. As we go along making these heart-wrenching decisions, one at a time, we pack items in a third group that we don't need or want and give them to Goodwill, the Salvation Army, a church outreach program or another charity. Finally, we toss out things that no longer have value for anyone.

For some reason, it is mothers who usually start this task, and later they get the nod of approval or the disagreeing shake of the head from their husbands on their specific decisions. Sometimes it helps to sort out our child's possessions with a friend or another family member. Having that emotional support can be a big help, especially having someone to share the stories about the items we are packing or to help us decide which box to put them in.

Sometimes we simply want to be by ourselves. We need to cry our eyes out and have that special time alone to let the floodgates open. We might be able to accomplish only a little each day. It could take hours just to read the letters and cards we find. Some decisions are so hard to make that we start another pile, which we call "I'm not sure." For example, it is devastating to throw out drivers' licenses, credit cards, school IDs, Social Security cards—all the documents that announced proudly who your child was—even though you know you will have no practical use for them.

Don't let anyone bully you into making snap decisions about your child's possessions. Take your time, relive all the memories, and have a good cry. Most importantly, make sure you don't let somebody clean out everything for you. Even though people who want to help might offer and you might very well want someone else to do this job, don't leave yourself without these memories and tangible objects to link you with your child.

Many of us fill boxes with things we can't part with. Most of us stash them, all nicely labeled, in the attic or other storage area. Occasionally or once a year we will open the boxes, and little by little over the years we are able to dispose of some things that have lost their heart-hold on us. As the years go by our favorite things might fit into one precious box, which we would take to our grave with us. Why do we get so attached to these things? They are the spark for rekindling our memories, our permanent link with our child.

We confront different hurdles if our child did not live with us or was married. Packing up what belonged to them often involves deciding what is worth hauling back to our home and finding space for it, and we may have to do it more quickly than we wish to avoid paying extra months' rent. Sometimes a relative or close friend might volunteer to box things up for us, relieving us of the task, especially if our child lived far away. (My cousin and her husband, who lived about an hour's drive from Peggy's college in Ohio, thoughtfully offered to pack up her belongings that were in the campus house she shared, saving me a very traumatic trip to Ohio that I was in no shape to make. The only things I asked to have sent to me were her papers, books and personal items; I invited her grieving roommates to keep the pots and pans and dishes and any clothes of Peggy's they would like to have. When that trunk arrived at our home it was one more traumatic task to face, but at least it was at home and not in Ohio, far from the loving arms of my support system.)

If your child was married, most likely his or her spouse will honor your requests to keep a few possessions, perhaps even seeking your help sorting out your child's things. If you have a strained relationship with your child's spouse or partner and are offered little or nothing, you might console yourself by adopting Mother Teresa's philosophy of being content with only a few material things. Sometimes letters or pictures saved over the years are the only lasting possessions you have to treasure. If so, be grateful that you have them.

> *The fear that we will forget details about our child haunts many of us bereaved parents.*

One bereaved couple, who lost their 29-year-old son in a drowning accident, bought a trendy rattan trunk and put it in their living room. They chose meaningful items from their son's life and placed them in the trunk. In an instant they are ready to share these treasured items with anyone who visits their home. They feel the everyday comfort of having his things nearby in a place of honor. Some parents living in apartments and condos where space is limited or who have only a few of their child's possessions find this idea a great solution for housing the precious things that belonged to their child. It becomes a centerpiece of conversation, sparking welcome comments and stories about their child.

Savoring memories

The fear that we will forget details about our child haunts many of us bereaved parents. We want to remember every little thing that made our child unique. Many of us turn to our photo albums or boxes of pictures we have stashed away and quickly assemble the best snapshots of our children into new albums dedicated to them. We desperately search for the picture that stirs our heart, the one with the likeness we most want to freeze in our mind. Those of us whose children had closed caskets know how much the one special picture we placed on top of the casket meant to us.

Most of us select a few favorite photos and spend a lot of time and money on framing that first year. But those pictures answer something in our soul. They greet us "Good morning," and they bid us "Good night." (One of my dearest friends, who was also a bereaved mother, took favorite pictures of Peggy and Denis and designed a screensaver for my computer—something so simple but so moving. Even to this day, every time I turn on the computer up pop Peggy and Denis smiling at me, and each night I shut down the computer I blow them a kiss goodnight, feeling like I am tucking them in as a good mother would. Today, as my little grandson passes by my computer— and remember, he never met either of them—he points to their pictures and says, "Aunt Peggy and Uncle Denis!" Do you know what that does for my heart?)

> *One of my dearest friends took favorite pictures of Peggy and Denis and designed a screensaver for my computer.*

My Peggy died a short time after having her sorority picture taken at college by one of those school photo companies. It wasn't the best picture of her because she was sporting a new perm that was not her normal hairdo. I didn't order any copies of the picture, even though it had her beautiful smile and her twinkling eyes in glorious color and her famous dimple on the chin ("A dimple in the chin, the devil within" goes an Irish proverb that we quoted a lot.) After her funeral I wrote to the company and asked if I could change my mind and told them why. And God bless them, they sent me a whole package, 11 x 14's, 5 x 7's and two full pages of pocket photos—at no charge. I was touched by their kindness. So Peggy's face, still adorned with that un-Peggy-like perm, graces my bureau. It's the last solo picture taken of her.

I was a sentimental saver (my husband might say "pack rat"). I kept all the cards my children made or bought and sent to me over the years, from when they could barely print their first name in kindergarten to the letters they wrote from college. Going through those after Peggy and Denis died produced lots of warm, fuzzy memories and buckets of tears. That was the toughest box I had to go through, much harder than the clothes. I didn't throw out a single piece of paper. I just sat and reread them all. To this day, looking over those priceless cards and letters still brings tears to my eyes and a lump to my throat as I picture Peggy and Denis saying each word—especially the apologies after they had done something wrong.

We bereaved parents constantly find unique ways to keep memories alive. That thought is uppermost in our mind. It's as if we are in a giant think tank, exploring new and better ways to have our child remembered. For example, designing vanity license plates with our child's name, age, birth date, nickname, favorite team or cause hidden in them brings us comfort each day as we drive along proclaiming to the world that we won't forget our child. "ANDY 18" and "DONORMOM" are license plates that are constant reminders of a precious child who died too young. Even bumper stickers such as "I brake for butterflies" or e-mail addresses such as "OurAngel" and "BttrflyMom" are used to declare a parent's love.

Even more creative are the Web sites bereaved parents have set up in memory of their children, offering their child's story, poignant poetry, helpful articles, grief resources, book reviews, conference notices, and links to other Web sites. The hours of work grieving parents spend on them gives them a focus, and the sites are a way for them to express their feelings. Some bereaved parents find solace sharing their memories via special Internet chat rooms designed for bereaved parents who desperately want to know how to survive and need friendship and understanding from other grieving parents. They find a tremendous healing being able to talk about their child and share their hopes and fears. In areas with no local support groups, these chat rooms have been a Godsend.

Address labels offer another unique way to keep our child remembered. Combining our child's picture with our address and affixing it to each envelope we mail announces that our child lived and that we are sharing this special person with the recipient. It's a little gesture, but it has a big impact on us every time we stick one on an envelope. It feels good to see our child being part of our everyday living.

Another popular trend among bereaved parents is wearing a necklace with their child's picture hanging from it, framed in an open locket or etched on a hologram. Both fathers and mothers proudly wear them, so happy to keep their precious child's face right in front of the public. How happy they are to evoke conversation about their child. It is especially poignant to see fathers who never before cared to wear jewelry proudly sporting one of these necklaces.

Many costume jewelry pins offer a frame for a child's picture, allowing us to subtly announce our child's presence. Putting a favorite snapshot inside the frame allows us to feel the nearness of our child in those dark beginning days when our child feels so far away. Angel pins of many styles also offer a touching way to remember our child. I have been gifted with many of these, but my favorite one is of two golden angels; it adorns almost every outfit I wear. It gives my heart great pleasure, makes me feel I take Peggy and Denis everywhere with me, and announces so beautifully the fact that I am angelically connected to them.

Investing that special love

One thing for sure: We do not want to waste that special love we have for our child solely in grieving. It takes a while for us to realize we can use it in other ways, and then it takes even more time to figure out just how we will put it to work in a meaningful way. When we put that love to good use, it's called *reinvestment*. It's a powerful feeling to know that our love for our child makes a difference in the world. Reinvestment—celebrating our children's lives by doing things for others in their memory—begins a whole new life for us. While we are helping ourselves by remembering our child, we are also helping others, which is a double blessing in our life.

Many of us begin right at the funeral by requesting that in lieu of flowers people make a donation to a charity of their choice or a designated fund. We established a memorial scholarship at the University of Dayton, first in Peggy's name and then adding Denis' name so as not to separate the memories of our "inseparable duo." Sometimes just keeping track of the paperwork and thanking donors to the fund gave us a reason to get out of bed in the morning in those early days. Knowing that some good was coming out of their terrible deaths was a lift to our hearts.

A lot of us establish scholarships at the schools our children attended. The scholarships keep us connected to a place they loved and insure that their name remains on the school programs each year as the awards are announced. Some of us have outfitted entire rooms in their schools; added to library supplies and computer rooms; or donated money for daycare toys and materials, musical instruments or sports equipment.

One family funded the refurbishing of a classroom as a mock courtroom for various high school social studies and justice programs. They could picture their 16-year-old son emoting in front of the judge's bench or even being the judge. (In a real "Perry Mason" atmosphere, this new room allows a peer jury to deliver peer punishment for school infractions. How their son would have loved that!)

Another family donated new stage curtains for the elementary school auditorium, remembering how their daughter always complained about the ugly, ripped, faded ones.

Another family donated new stage curtains for the elementary school auditorium, remembering how their daughter always complained about the ugly, ripped, faded ones that were hard to open and close for their class plays. Thinking "what would my child like" prompted another set of bereaved parents to set up a fund to raise money for new band instruments to replace the beat-up ones their son had refused to bring home. Listening to the concerts with the new flutes and clarinets brought smiles to their faces, as the parents remembered renting a used instrument and nagging their son to practice. They became involved in publicity and scheduling for the band and orchestra, giving them a focus and a special way to remember their child with the music he loved.

A bereaved mom who lost her only child the night before high school graduation in a car accident faithfully wrote a monthly newsletter, "Lamentations," that she mailed to hun-

dreds of bereaved parents across the United States until ill
health forced her to discontinue it. However, she continues to
host an annual picnic for these families at Cumberland College
in Kentucky, where they get to meet each other, share their stories, and hear inspiring speakers. One of the first people she
helped, a bereaved mom who lost two
teenage sons in an automobile accident, calls each newly bereaved parent
she hears about. She offers friendly
support and mails them a special
packet containing favorite articles,
books and videos to help their grieving. She sent packets to as many
bereaved parents as she could locate
who lost a child from the 1996 TWA
Flight 800 plane crash; the World Trade Center offices of Can-
tor Fitzgerald, a firm that lost hundreds of employees in the
9/11 attack; and from our war with Iraq. She attaches personal
notes and asks the families to send her a picture of their child,
which she places in albums next to their name. As much as she
loves seeing the faces of these children, their parents are
delighted to share them with someone. What love this woman
invests as she "sings the songs" of her two boys.

*This dome is a
visual gift to the
bereaved families
who converge on
the campus for a
reunion every June.*

This same woman and her husband funded the painting of
a dome in the lobby of the newly built inn at Cumberland College in 1994. They commissioned an artist to paint colorful
cherubs and symbols (butterfly, horse, basketball, guitar) on the
dome, representing some of the deceased children of the
bereavement group that meets annually at the college. Then
she compiled the stories of 28 of these children in a book entitled *Children of the Dome,* of which Peggy and Denis are a part.
This dome is a visual gift to the bereaved families who converge
on the campus for a reunion every June and for the college students and visitors who enjoy the facilities of the inn. It is a constant reminder of beautiful lives that ended all too early.

Another bereaved mother and father lost their only child,
a daughter who was almost 16, and now edit and send out a
special newsletter called "Alive Alone," focused specifically on

parents who have lost their only child or only children. This mom also presents conference workshops sharing how to cope and survive the loss of an only child—a very devastating loss with the added pain of having no other child remaining to nurture and love.

A mother who lost her 16-year-old son to suicide wrote a booklet sharing her son's story and the excruciating pain his death brought her family. She felt that if the booklet's message would deter one person from taking his or her life and a family from a lifetime of agony then her son would not have died in vain. Other bereaved parents have gone on to be telephone buddies, write newsletters and books, facilitate support groups, present workshops, sponsor seminars and conferences, and be directors of national support organizations such as The Compassionate Friends, Mothers Against Drunk Driving and Parents of Murdered Children. All these grieving parents want to share what they have learned to make the journey easier for the newly bereaved.

Other families set up funds or foundations for art, music and dance lessons; sports camps; computer classes; or other hobbies or sports their child loved. A few families have sponsored the training of a puppy candidate as a seeing–eye dog in memory of children who were dog lovers. Some sponsor boating and fishing trips for the disabled, honoring their children who were outdoors types and environment lovers. Others devote themselves to working for the Special Olympics, something they used to do together with their child. One family sponsored a traveling art show featuring the artwork of the local schoolchildren in a community that suffered many losses in the World Trade Center tragedy. They organized the event, choosing the artwork and how it would be displayed, locating places and making a schedule for the exhibit, handling the publicity, and arranging for transportation and set-up of the exhibit. It was a labor of love that helped children who had lost a family member in the tragedy, as well as their classmates, to express their sadness.

Some parents have donated a collection of children's books to their local library or school, choosing their child's favorite books or books on a subject their child loved. Others fund school programs, bringing informative seminars, exciting musical events and interesting guest speakers to enrich the youngsters' studies—all in the name of their child.

Because their son loved Christmas, one family donated a life-size angel for the new crèche displayed on the altar of their church. They felt as if their son was standing right there at the manger, wings and all—a joyful part of their holy day celebration.

Many of us share our special love by volunteering with advocacy groups. Whether we are canvassing our neighborhood for donations to Cancer Care, tying red ribbons on car antennas for Mothers Against Drunk Driving, sewing patches for AIDS quilts, or stuffing envelopes for the American Foundation for Suicide Prevention, we are pouring our energies into a worthy cause in memory of our child, and that is healing. Some of us volunteer at nursing homes, hospitals or senior centers to bring cheer or special programs to these folks. One bereaved mom brings volunteers from her Garden Club to share their flower-arranging skills with the residents at the local nursing home. She even talked the local funeral home into saving her some lovely flowers each week for this venture. Lugging greenery, flowers, utensils and materials, she and her volunteers are the highlight of the week for many of the elderly, lonely souls who attend. Some patients are thrilled for the opportunity to converse in a few words of their native tongue as this bereaved mom chats with them in Italian. She returns home with a full heart, knowing she has made somebody else's day better. It's a good feeling to be caught up in your volunteer work, letting those long hours zoom by while you help someone else who might need a lift even more than you.

A number of bereaved parents offer their talents to help support groups such as The Compassionate Friends. One mother brings all the cake, coffee and paper goods for our monthly meetings—with a smile—doing it in memory of her 21-year-old daughter. With her car trunk filled with supplies, she makes us laugh when she calls her car "Compassionate Friends on wheels." Another mom arrives early at each meeting to set up the boxes of books for our Lending Library in memory of the beautiful 35-year-old daughter she lost to cancer. Another dedicated mom phones each of the new members to welcome them after each meeting in memory of her 32-year-old son who died in a plane crash. Each month four dads (one is my husband Joe) set up the chairs and tables, lug the boxes of library books and supplies from the storage closet, and fill the large coffee pots for our meetings—all investing their special love for their deceased children. Another couple picks up the newsletter at the printer each month, folds and staples it, puts on the labels and stamps and takes it to the post office for mailing in memory of their 22-year-old son. Every time I answer the phone and answer people's questions or give them information about the next meeting, I feel Peggy and Denis smiling down on me approvingly.

Some parents get busy beautifying a special area in their town in honor of their child.

Some days, when I plan to go to the cemetery but don't make it because of some involvement or work that needs to be done, I feel sure they understand I was using that time helping somebody.

Others have turned to Scouting, 4-H, coaching sports teams, or teaching religious education or Sunday school classes in memory of their child. They like being surrounded by children and maybe making a difference for a child who needs a caring adult in their life. Knowing we are sharing that special love we have for our child with other children is a great motivator for getting bereaved parents involved and doing something positive.

Some parents get busy beautifying a special area in their town in honor of their child. Whether it's an empty lot, a roadway or the village green, they love the hard work of digging, chopping, pruning, mowing, sweeping, lugging and planting. They spend months designing what they will include on the site, weeks incorporating their plan, and years maintaining the area—always thinking of their child as they throw themselves wholeheartedly into the loving project. Other parents plant a tree, and sometimes a grove of trees, in the local park, at a school, at their church or in a support group garden. These trees offer natural beauty, perpetual growth and welcoming shade to others in their child's memory. In 1992 our Compassionate Friends group wanted to plant trees in the local park for a program the county was offering, but due to

For some of us, sharing our child's love means doing random acts of kindness.

staff layoffs the program fizzled. I asked the director of buildings and grounds at Molloy College, where we meet every month, if they could use some landscaping for their new academic building. The response was an emphatic "Yes!" We planted 333 trees and shrubs surrounding the entire building—a $15,000 labor of love—just in time to celebrate our fifth anniversary on their campus. It was a great way to say "thank you" for offering us such a wonderful safe haven for our meetings—and years later we're still there.

For some of us, sharing our child's love means doing random acts of kindness. It could be as simple as holding a door, helping someone cross the street, picking up a dinner check for the elderly gentleman sitting alone in the restaurant, or gifting a few people in line at the movie theater with tickets. (Always accompany such gestures with a little card that states something like "An Act of Kindness in memory of..." with your child's name and date of birth and death printed on it. You will see from the expression on people's faces that they feel as if they were visited by an angel.)

People say to me, "Isn't it nice that after all these years that Peggy and Denis still make a difference in the world?" Sharing that special love I have for them *does* make a difference in the world—and in my heart too! You can experience that same wonderful feeling as you invest the special love you have for your child in ways that are meaningful to you. Then you can learn—as I have—that the more of God's love we accept, the more of God's love we are called to express.

Growing fully alive through the gifts of loss

After one door closes does another one open? Does anything good come from our terrible loss? Are there really gifts to be found in the death of our child? Do we have to look for these gifts, or do they just appear? Do they come announced with a flare of trumpets, or do they gently sneak into our heart as part of the new person we are becoming? Will we find life is worth living? Can we feel alive again?

Our lives have changed and we have changed—there is no doubt about that. Our grief has caused us to take a closer look at ourselves. Through our meditations, prayer or journaling, insights about ourselves have been revealed to us that we never realized before. Seeing things clearly, in the true light of God's love, is a gift. We see possibilities and open doors we had not seen before. We discover what drives us crazy and what mellows us out. After dealing with the death of our child, we are more open to expressing ourselves, to understanding our feelings, to sharing them, to forgiving ourselves and others. We are not so concerned with the "right" way but with whatever way is right for us. We learn to be gentle with ourselves, to take time for ourselves. We take things "one day at a time" or "one hour at a time." Eventually we come to know in our heart that we did the best we could with what we had. We accept ourselves with all our shortcomings.

We feel stronger, more resilient, more capable, more adaptable than we ever imagined ourselves to be. After surviving the death of our child, we feel that we could take on the world, since we have already dealt with the worst thing that could ever happen to us. A new sense of empowerment fills our being. We are ready for whatever the future holds. We find joy in enhancing the lives of people around us. Our outlook gives others hope. Our hand reaches out to other bereaved parents and is a catalyst for their recovery.

We experience emotions we didn't know existed. We are on our way to learning a new language of feelings. Our child's death teaches us to dig deep into our inner resources, and we surprise ourselves with the range of emotions we experience.

Crying and being sad, feeling as low as we can possibly feel, helps us appreciate our capacity for moments of joy and positive feelings of love and gratitude. The more familiar love and joy become to us, the more easily we handle anger, confusion and hopelessness. How wonderful it is to discover we are richer because we now have more emotional skills to deal with everyday life.

The death of our child leads us to reassess the priorities in our life. We seem to have a clearer understanding of what's important, what's transient and what's irrelevant. We rediscover enduring values that we would not give up for anything in the world. We focus more strongly on the values that sustain and comfort us. We decide to spend more time with our family, to rekindle that spark with our spouse, to cut back on work hours, to take a leave of absence, to travel, to visit relatives we haven't seen in a while, to take up a new hobby, to reconnect with our faith, to be gentle with ourselves, to embrace new friendships, to further our education, or even to stop our self-destructive behavior. We change the direction of our life, reorganize ourselves, and enjoy the new person we are becoming due to the death of our child. In our grief, we grow to become a new and better person.

I fought becoming a new person with a vengeance. I wanted to remain the "old me." I liked the old me; my husband fell in love with the old me—my effervescence, my optimism, my laughter. But how foolish I was, thinking I could stay the same person after such a traumatic experience. My whole body had been assaulted, my heart broken, and my mind left to deal with it all. Fighting and kicking all the way, a "new me" emerged with rearranged priorities and deeper feelings. I scaled down my commitments and I loved my husband twice as much. A leaky pipe, a flat tire, a fender-bender, a late airplane no longer fazed me. They seemed so trivial in comparison to what I had endured.

We discover (or rediscover) the presence of God in ways that might be new to us or through the old, familiar, comfortable ways we've always enjoyed. We choose to believe there is an order and purpose to our lives, even if we don't have all the answers. We believe we are part of something much deeper than we can understand. Our faith allows us to accept our loss more easily, believing there is an order, a purpose, a divine plan that will make sense to us someday—if not here, then in the glory of the hereafter. (I keep telling myself the Lord will explain it all to me someday.)

It seems spirituality has a powerful effect in helping people recover a sense of balance, tranquility and hope.

Many of us attending support groups observe that the bereaved parents who lean into their faith for support deal better with their loss. It seems spirituality has a powerful effect in helping people recover a sense of balance, tranquility and hope. We haven't found any medical technology or psychological process that equals the power of faith. Believing we are held in the hands of the Lord—that he is always with us, ever listening to our heartache—provides a real comfort that is one of the best gifts we receive from our loss.

Riding the roller coaster of grief, we are familiar with its ups and downs. We learn to face hard times head-on. We don't scoot around them or hide from them. We experience real growth as we struggle through pain, confusion, sadness, anger, guilt, fear, depression and uncertainty. We learn the value of patience, of taking care of ourselves, of having loving listeners and a strong support system. Slowly, step by step, we learn what we can control and what we can't change. We develop and mature. We experience the gift of growth.

Right now we are role models, whether we realize it or not. Others are watching us. We can be an inspiration to them, encouraging them to take a step at a time, have patience with themselves, go at their own pace, and take good care of themselves. Because others are learning from our experience, we are teachers. When people learn that I have lost two children, they seem to say to themselves, "If she's still standing up after losing two children, maybe I can make it too." By helping others, we are making the world a little better place. We have the satisfaction of knowing that our child's life continues to make a difference in the world, changing it in little ways.

The gifts of loss bring joy to our heart and an inner peace to our whole being. Our decisions, actions and responses echo our faith in God and God's ever-present guidance. We feel safe and secure, blessed with renewed life and vitality as we grow into the new person we are becoming.

I give you thanks, O Lord, with my whole heart....
On the day I called, you answered me,
you increased my strength of soul.

Psalm 138:1,3

Living the Promise of the Resurrection

I am the resurrection and the life.
Those who believe in me, even though they die, will live,
and everyone who lives and believes in me will never die.

John 11:25-26

For Christian parents who have lost a child, the joyful promise of the Resurrection delights our heart and renews our spirit. The thought that we will be reunited with our precious child (or children) fills us with an overwhelming sense of peace and invites us to live fully in the here and now. It encourages us to rediscover the richness of life. It makes us feel more strongly connected to our friends, family, church and the world around us; sharpens our senses; clarifies our perceptions. The Resurrection allows love to be our driving force. We feel the transformation it brings and passionately want to share the wonder of it with others.

The glorious promise of the Resurrection is an overflowing source of energy for us bereaved parents. It opens our heart to new horizons, inviting new good into our life. It prompts us to use all our faculties, powers and talents to express our human potential in every situation. It makes us appreciate the smiles and laughter that bubble forth from God's joy. It gives us our new zest for life, helping us experience some joy despite our pain. It lets us feel an inner peace by uniting us with others and wrapping us closely in God's loving embrace. It reminds us that through every challenge and blessing God is our constant guide and companion. It prompts us to perceive the beauty around us, to treasure simplicity, to realize what we're here for.

The promise of the Resurrection also develops our sense of wonder. We begin to notice epiphanies in everything. We find meaning in our lives and in our work. We find endless possibilities for doing good deeds. We turn control over to God and develop trust in his goodness and love. We discover that a whole new level of living awaits our willingness to release the old and welcome the new. We affirm that God will show us what to do.

The promise that we will someday be in glory together with our child recharges our batteries, allowing us to fulfill the purpose for which we are here. Our dreams take wings and our worries surrender. We move forward, secure in the understanding that we are in the flow of the divine order. We expand our thinking and deepen our insights. We wake up each morning ready to receive. We don't predict how we will be blessed; we just let it unfold naturally.

As we accept the promise of the Resurrection, our life is transformed. Little by little we become aware of the positive feelings that gently give us the strength to go on. Everything happens subtly, in little increments. Our hearts feel stronger, we are able to accomplish more, we smile more, we deal better with people. The pain lessens, though it will always be a sacred part of us. We feel the serenity of God in each step we take, sensing our child's presence as part of the Communion of Saints. We gratefully reach for life and determinedly find the purpose we are destined to serve.

When I envision heaven, I see Peggy's and Denis' beaming faces and the faces of my babies lost through miscarriage. My heart is overwhelmed with tears of joy as I patiently await our glorious reunion. Every day we are one day closer!

May God's blessings accompany you on your journey of grief. May you have a day of resurrection, feeling restored in mind and body, reviving your commitment to pursue your hopes and dreams, renewing your enthusiasm for life and for doing what adds meaning and purpose to your life. This will be the ultimate gift of love to your child.

I have heard your prayer, I have seen your tears;
indeed, I will heal you.

2 Kings 20:5

Acknowledgments

The Lord's plan is amazing. Filled with never-ending surprises, it keeps unfolding, gracing my life with beautiful people, happy events, and exciting opportunities. With a grateful heart, I thank the Lord and these special people he placed in my life for their healing presence, loving support, and endless encouragement. They all played an integral part in my journey, leading to the writing of this book, a dream come true for me.

Thanks to my dearest friends, whose caring carried me through the darkest hours of my grief and whose love continues to fill my heart today: Virginia Antakli, Nancy Rusch, Serena Hubbell, Ann Allen-Cetrino, Elaine Vlahos, Lynne Fallon and Catherine Olsen; and to my cousin, Gail Gallagher, who accompanied me on the journey.

Thanks to all my Compassionate Friends, who walk the walk with me, especially: Sue and John Arleo, Elaine and Jerry Good, Yolanda and Angelo Damiani, Diane and John Scotton, Connie and Bob Purick, Anne Marie Maiorana and Martha Weiss, all adding their hard earned wisdom to this book and supporting me with their confidence and enthusiasm.

Thanks to my Kentucky friend, Rosemary Smith, who bonded instantly with me after the deaths of her two oldest children and who shares an incredible grief journey with me as we collaborate to reach out to the newly bereaved across the United States.

Thanks to my media friends, inviting me to do seminars, documentaries, and television programs for the bereaved with them: "Fr. Tom" Hartman, George Anderson, Andrew Barone, and Frank Smith; and to Melissa and David Schwartz for helping my videos reach so many hurting families.

Thanks to my publishing friends and role models who have guided me along my literary path of writing for the bereaved, Joy Johnson and Janet Sieff of Centering Corporation, Andrea Gambill of Grief Digest, and Hans Christofferson of Liguori Publications.

Thanks to my National Catholic Ministry to the Bereaved (NCMB) friends, especially my mentor and fellow ACTA Publications author, Sister Mauryeen O'Brien, OP, whose confidence in me led to the birth of this book; and to Dick Gilbert, always ready with a gazillion resources, super ideas, sparkling humor, and a helping hand.

Thanks to my Family Ministry friends, who affirm my work with the bereaved, especially the late Dr. Patrick Del Zoppo, who invited me to be diocesan bereavement coordinator, and Sister Lauren Hanley, CSJ, who daily validates my work with her total support of my programs.

Thanks to my editor, Todd Behme, my new friend, whose understanding heart, rich literary skills, and painstaking efforts enhanced the healing message of my manuscript.

Thanks to my friendly publisher, Greg Pierce, who believed in my story and gave me the opportunity to share what I have learned with other bereaved parents.

And lastly my special thanks to my loving husband, Joe, to whom I feel joined at the hip, since his constant help allows me to do so much more as we work together; and to my daughter Annie, for her patience and understanding, sharing me with so many bereaved families.

About the Author

Wife, mother, grandmother, educator, author and speaker, Elaine E. Stillwell shares her gifts of hope and inspiration with the bereaved, simply telling what she has learned to cope and survive following the deaths of her two oldest children. She is the author of two crafts books for bereaved children, *Sweet Memories* and *A Forever Angel*, and two pamphlets for bereaved adults, *Healing After Your Child's Death* and *Stepping Stones for the Bereaved*. She is a contributing editor for *Grief Digest* and is founder and Chapter Leader of The Compassionate Friends of Rockville Centre and the Bereavement Coordinator for Ministry to Families of the Diocese of Rockville Centre, New York.

Additional Grief Resources from ACTA Publications

We Were Gonna Have a Baby,
But We Had an Angel Instead
Pat Schwiebert
Illustrated by Taylor Bills
A special book for children who have recently lost a sibling-to-be, narrated by a young boy who shares his and his family's disappointment and grief over a miscarriage or loss of his baby brother or sister. Includes a section of helpful information on how to help grieving children. (24-page four-color paperback, $7.95)

The New Day Journal
A Journey from Grief to Healing
Mauryeen O'Brien, OP
Designed to help those mourning the loss of a loved one work their way through the four tasks of grief: accepting the reality of the loss, experiencing the pain of grief, adjusting to change, and creating memories and goals. Uses prayer, reflection, questions, readings and journaling. (96-page workbook, $9.95)

Lift Up Your Hearts
Meditations for Those Who Mourn
Mauryeen O'Brien, OP
Over forty complete personal prayer experiences. Psalm verses and scripture passages combined with reflections, questions and prayers connect a grieving person with the spirit of the healing Lord. (112-page paperback, $9.95)

Hidden Presence
Twelve Blessings That Transformed Sorrow or Loss
Edited by Gregory F. Augustine Pierce
A collection of true stories of blessings that somehow transformed a sorrow or loss. Each of the twelve storytellers in this book recalls a very real benefit or insight gained from a tragedy, failure, illness or disaster in his or her life. (176-page hardcover gift book with silver ribbon, $17.95)

Tear Soup
A Recipe for Healing After Loss
Pat Schwiebert and Chuck DeKlyen
Illustrated by Taylor Bills
Voted the best children's book of 2001 by the Association of Theological Booksellers, this modern-day fable tells the story of a woman who has suffered a terrible loss and must cook up a special batch of "tear soup" in order to grieve. Richly illustrated, for children and adults alike. (56-page hardcover gift book, $19.95; 24-minute VHS video, $24.95)

Available from booksellers or call 800-397-2282
www.actapublications.com